Listening _to_ God
Day by Day

SHARON JAYNES

To Deb

Sharon Jaynes

HARVEST HOUSE PUBLISHERS

EUGENE, OREGON

Cover by Dugan Design Group, Bloomington, Minnesota

Cover photo © artjazz / Fotolia

LISTENING TO GOD DAY BY DAY
Formerly titled *Extraordinary Moments with God* with additions and revisions
Copyright © 2008/2011 by Sharon Jaynes
Published by Harvest House Publishers
Eugene, Oregon 97402
www.harvesthousepublishers.com

Library of Congress Cataloging-in-Publication Data
Jaynes, Sharon.
Listening to God day by day / Sharon Jaynes.
    p. cm.
Rev. ed. of: Extraordinary moments with God.
Includes bibliographical references.
ISBN 978-0-7369-3870-9 (pbk.)
1. Devotional literature. 2. Meditations. I. Jaynes, Sharon. Extraordinary moments with God. II. Title.
BV4832.3.J39 2011
242'.5—dc23
                                                                2011016826

Printed in the United States of America

11 12 13 14 15 16 17 18 19 / VP-SK / 10 9 8 7 6 5 4 3 2 1

This book is dedicated to my son, Steven.

*One of my most extraordinary moments with God
was when you were placed in my arms in the delivery room.*

What a joy it is to be your mom.

I love you...more.

Gentle Whispers, Tender Tugs

Does God still speak today? Does God speak to you and to me? Oh, yes, dear friend. God still speaks, and He is speaking to both of us. The question is…will we listen?

The very first question in the Bible was asked by an all-knowing God (Genesis 3:9). "Where are you?" He asked Adam and Eve, who hid in the bushes, ashamed of how they had disobeyed God's one and only command. He didn't ask because He didn't know where Adam and Eve were, but because He wanted them to come out of hiding and meet with Him face-to-face. He wanted to speak to them.

All through the Bible we see God speaking to His children. Sometimes face-to-face, but more often He spoke through nature, circumstances, other people, and celestial beings. Tell me, haven't you longed for God to speak to you in the same way?

Admittedly, it is hard to hear anyone's voice surrounded by the cacophony of noises in our busy world where the TV is blaring, the radio is booming, the washing machine is spinning, the vacuum cleaner is roaring, the kids are yelling, the dog is barking, the baby is crying, the telephone is ringing, and the doorbell is buzzing—all at the same time. I've often thought, *If I could just get away from the clamor and calamity of everyday life, perhaps I could hear that still, small voice.* But when I pored over the pages of Scripture, I discovered that some of God's most memorable messages were not delivered while men and women were away at a spiritual retreat, but right in the middle of the hustle and bustle of everyday life. He spoke to Moses while he was tending sheep, to Gideon while he was threshing wheat, to shepherds while they were watching their flocks by night, to Zechariah while he was performing his duties at the temple, to Peter and Andrew while they were fishing on the sea, to the woman at the well while she was drawing water for her household chores, to Matthew while he was working in his tax office, and to Martha while she was cooking in the kitchen.

Does that mean that God can speak to you and to me in the midst of our ordinary days? I don't believe it is a question of whether or not He will speak, but whether or not we will listen. In *Experiencing God*, Henry Blackaby said: "Right now God is working all around you and in your life. One of the greatest tragedies among God's people is that, while they have a deep longing to experience God, they are experiencing God day after day but do not know how to recognize Him."*

There are some who say God does not speak today, that the Bible is God's complete revelation to believers. Yes, it is true that the Bible tells us everything we need to know about God's character and His ways, and He will never tell us anything that contradicts His Word. But He will also speak to us in a personal way to help us apply Scripture to our lives and move the truths from our heads to our hearts.

All through the New Testament Jesus taught the multitudes by telling them stories or parables to illustrate spiritual principles. He explained the unknown by using the known. Jesus said, "The kingdom of heaven is like a man who sowed good seed in his field" (Matthew 13:27). "The kingdom of heaven is like a mustard seed" (Matthew 13:31). "The kingdom of God is like treasure hidden in a field" (Matthew 13:44). "The kingdom of God is like a net that was let down into the lake and caught all kinds of fish" (Matthew 13:47). Likewise, Jesus continues to illustrate spiritual principles through modern-day parables. He shows up in our lives every day, but like Moses, who "turned aside" to look at the burning bush (Exodus 3:2 NASB), we must turn aside and pay attention. I wonder how many burning bushes I've missed in my own backyard because I've been too busy. I fear we have grown unaccustomed to listening, uninterested in what He has to say or unbelieving He will speak at all.

Does God still speak to us today? I'm absolutely sure He does. But don't take my word for it—take Jesus'. He said, "I am the good

---

* Henry T. Blackaby and Claude V. King, *Experiencing God* (Nashville, TN: The Sunday School Board of the Southern Baptist Convention, 1990), 15.

shepherd...My sheep listen to my voice; I know them and they follow me" (John 10:14,27). I haven't heard God's audible voice, but He does speak to me on a regular basis. I've felt His nudge in the kitchen as I've mopped the dirty floor, I've recognized His tug as I've pulled off the highway in an overheated car, I've sensed His peaceful wooing as I've struggled to weather tumultuous storms, I've learned His lessons as I've sat stranded in crowded airports, I've heard echoes of His laughter as He's instructed me to learn from the children in my care—parables all. But most importantly, I've heard God speak to my heart through the pages of my well-worn Bible.

I hope you have read my book *Becoming a Woman Who Listens to God* and learned how to tune your spiritual senses to the frequency of God's voice. In this devotion book, we will be putting those principles into practice by listening to God right in the middle of our busy lives. We'll see the miraculous smack-dab in the middle of the mundane. In each entry we'll have a Bible passage to ponder, a parable to paint a picture, and a prayer to unite our hearts with God's. Join me now as we listen to God in the nooks and crannies of our everyday lives.

Earth is crammed with heaven,
And every common bush afire with God,
But only he who sees takes off his shoes.
ELIZABETH BARRETT BROWNING

Old Enough to Learn

Teach me your way, O Lord,
and I will walk in your truth.

PSALM 86:11

The little girl bounced up and down, trying to see over the bank counter as her daddy made a deposit. She was about three feet tall and not quite big enough to get a clear view.

"How old are you?" the teller asked.

The little girl stood up straight and tall and said, "I'm four years old, and next year I'm going to be five, and then I'll be old enough to learn!"

Of course we know she'd been learning her entire life. Being five just meant she could go to school.

Then God reminded me that sometimes His children put off learning about Him until...well, later. When the kids go off the school. When a big project is completed. When retirement rolls around. But the time for learning about God is *now*. All day God speaks to us through creation, other people, and our circumstances, but the primary way we learn about Him is through the pages of the Bible. He has written us an incredible love letter filled with precious promises, comforting commands, and godly guidelines just waiting to be discovered. The Hebrew word for "Bible" actually means, "The calling out of God." He is calling out to us from the pages of our Bibles. And we're never too young or too old to learn.

Because you're holding this book in your hand, I'm thinking you have decided that now is the time to learn. I'm right there with you, locking arms with you in this journey to become a woman who listens to God day by day to discover the abundant life Jesus came to give.

Dear Lord, thank You for teaching me. Help me to become a diligent student of Your Word who uncovers treasures on every page of Scripture. Open my eyes to discover Your truths and my heart to apply them. In Jesus' name, amen.

ADDITIONAL SCRIPTURE READING: PSALM 86:1-17

The Spelling Train

When I am weak, then I am strong.

2 Corinthians 12:10

My hands were clammy. Beads of sweat formed on my brow. A familiar knot in the pit of my stomach threatened to push me toward the restroom, and my dry tongue began cleave to the roof of my mouth. It was 10:25 a.m. In just five more minutes the dreaded event would begin.

When I was in the first grade, the one academic exercise I feared more than any other was the spelling train. It was sheer torture—at least for me.

"Okay, students," Mrs. March would say. "Everyone pick up your chairs and move them over to the chalkboard. It's time for the spelling train."

Twenty first graders slipped their munchkin-sized chairs from their desks to form a semi-circle around our chief engineer. I always put mine at the end.

"Now remember the rules," she explained. "I am going to hold up a flash card. If you read the word correctly, you get to go to the front of the train. If you miss it, you have to go to the caboose."

She held up the cards one by one, and the class chugged along at a quick pace. Dog. Sally. Dick. Jane. Spot. Red. Blue. Mother. Stop. Run. Then it was my turn.

"Sharon, what is this word?"

Pause. Giggles.

Well, more often than not I had no idea. And when that happened, I would either guess wrong or sit in silence. I spent most of my time in the first grade spelling train in the caboose.

As the year progressed, I did move up into the passenger cars a few times, but usually I didn't stay there long enough to keep the seat warm.

There was one particular word that kept me from ever visiting the front of the train: T-h-e. So Mrs. March decided she was going to help me. For two weeks she made me wear a name tag that read "THE" plastered on my chest like the scarlet letter. I can still remember kids coming up to me on the playground, pointing at THE on my chest, and saying, "Hey, what's that? Why are you wearing that? Is your name The? Are you stupid?"

Eventually I did learn how to spell the word t-h-e, but that's not all I learned. I learned that I was stupid, not as smart as everybody else, and just not good enough. But you know what? That wasn't true. Those were lies from the enemy. And it took many years for God to hold me by the hand and help me see myself as He sees me: a uniquely created, dearly loved, completely forgiven, and totally accepted child of God who is capable of doing everything He has called me to do by the power of the Holy Spirit.

That was more than forty years ago, and now one of my greatest joys is stringing written words together. I've noticed that life has many unusual twists and turns when God is at the helm. He takes our greatest weaknesses and turns them into our grandest strengths. That's what happens when we turn our lives over to Him—we get out of the caboose and get to ride up with the Chief Engineer to places we never imagined possible. When we are weak, then He is strong.

Where are you in the train of life right now? If you're hiding in the caboose, listen closely and you just might hear God calling you up front where you belong.

Dear Heavenly Father, it's amazing to think of all You have done in my life. You have taken my greatest weaknesses and turned them into my greatest strengths. When I am weak, through the power of the Holy Spirit I am strong. Thank You for working in me and through me. And help me never to believe the lies of the enemy that say "I'm not enough" again. In Jesus' name, amen.

ADDITIONAL SCRIPTURE READING: 2 CORINTHIANS 11:1–12:10

Lessons from the Battlefield

*Our struggle is not against flesh and blood, but against the rulers,
against the authorities, against the powers of this dark world
and against the spiritual forces of evil in the heavenly realms.*

EPHESIANS 6:12

In my early years, I was a rough and rowdy tomboy who climbed trees, skipped rocks, and made skid marks on the asphalt with my glittery pink banana seat bike. My backyard was the envy of every kid in the neighborhood. It came equipped with a drainage ditch across the back border that separated us from a vacant, thickly wooded lot. The ditch tunneled beneath six city blocks through concrete pipes large enough to stand up in and walk through, and culminated in a very large crater we dubbed "The Canyon." How do I know you could stand up in them? You guessed. We did it.

To the kids in the neighborhood, the ditch was a virtual wonderland filled with all kinds of creepy, crawly critters to be discovered. I felt like the luckiest kid around to have such an attraction right in my own backyard.

On the other side of "The Canyon" lived another neighborhood that was a bit rougher than ours. We dubbed the boys who lived there the "Canyon Boys." Great animosity existed between the Canyon Boys and the boys in our neighborhood (of which I thought I was one).

One day the warring factions decided there was going to be a big rumble between the two. The time: 2:00 p.m. The place: the drainage ditch bordering my backyard. The weapon of choice: dirt clods.

We boys gathered in my yard on the east side of the ditch as the enemy gathered in the vacant lot on the west. We gathered our ammo, hunkered down behind mounds of dirt and trees, and waited for the first shot to be fired. Then it began. Clods of hardened mud flew left and right. At some point during this heated battle, I peeked out from behind a tree to throw a grenade, and something hit me square in the forehead. I wasn't sure what it was, but it didn't feel like dirt. As blood poured down my brow, I looked on the ground and saw the culprit. A brick.

"You cheated!" I yelled at the enemy forces.

Fearing I had suffered a fatal blow, the enemies ran for their lives. My buds ran to get my mom, and I was whisked away to the hospital. The doctor shaved a patch of hair from my forehead, sewed my skin back together, and placed a patch over the wound. Oh, it wasn't as nifty as a broken arm or a broken leg, but having your head split open by a rival was pretty cool.

Some of my hair never grew back in that spot, and I have a scar to remind me of a few facts about fighting foes.

1. The enemy cheats.
2. The enemy slings more than just dirt.
3. The enemy has great aim.
4. The enemy's attacks sometimes leave scars.
5. The enemy is not playing a game.

I don't fight with bullies anymore—at least, not the human kind. But I do have one nemesis that challenges me regularly. The Bible calls him the "great deceiver," "the accuser," "the devil," "the evil one." Interestingly, the same lessons I learned from that dirt clod fight apply to him today.

What about you? Do you know how to fight the spiritual battles in your life? Ephesians 6:10-20 is a great place to start.

⌣

Dear Lord, today I put on the full armor of God to stand against the enemy's schemes: the helmet of salvation, the belt of truth, the breastplate of righteousness, and the sandals of the gospel of peace. I also take up the shield of faith in one hand and the sword of the Spirit in the other. Now I'm ready to take my stand. In Jesus' name, amen.

ADDITIONAL SCRIPTURE READING: EPHESIANS 6:10-20

Grandma's Hands

She opens her arms to the poor
and extends her hands to the needy.

PROVERBS 31:20

On a shelf in my living room sits a black-and-white photograph of a young girl taken in the early 1900s. Her hair is pulled back with an oversized bow peeking from behind the edges of her head. Her dress is typical of the times, with puffed sleeves and a brimming lace collar resting on her shoulders. She isn't smiling, and she appears to be somewhat awkward, timid, and, I dare say, even afraid. This is a picture of Grandmother Anderson on her wedding day. She was 14 years old.

As I gaze at this amazing woman, who bore 12 children and miscarried 11 others, I am always drawn to her hands. Hanging uncomfortably at her side are hands that seem much too large for her petite frame. "Anderson hands," my mother calls them. I surmise that God must have known this little lady would need a big heart and big hands to embrace all that life would send her way.

Like Grandmother Anderson, all of us mothers need big hearts and big hands. Our hands grip the bed rail in pain in the delivery room and then gently caress a newborn for the first time. Before long, those hands are changing diapers, washing bottoms and faces, cleaning spit-up, wiping tears, rocking sleepyheads, and placing babies in a crib. Then they are holding a toddler's chubby hand and grabbing him to keep him out of harm's way. Tossing a ball, preparing holiday dinners, setting a festive table, tying packages for birthday parties and Christmas presents. Coloring and cutting out shapes in workbooks. Picking up leaves and bugs for collections.

Pushing a swing and letting go of a bike as a child first learns to peddle on his own. Sewing party dresses and mending torn baseball jerseys, washing scraped knees and spooning out medicine. Holding the sweaty palm of an awkward adolescent while dancing around the den, tying the knot of a necktie and pinning on a boutonniere for a first party. Writing letters to children away at camp, or folding hands in prayer asking for the Lord's protection while they are away. Tightly grasping the steering wheel while chauffeuring children from one place to the next or gripping the seat as a teen learns how to drive.

Hands that wave goodbye as a son drives off to college and hands that adjust a cherished daughter's wedding veil. A mother's hands are loving hands, disciplining hands, grieving hands, protecting hands, and providing hands. They embrace the child and then, when the child is ready, she opens them and lets them go.

Take a look at your hands today and ask God how He would have you use them.

Dear Lord, thank You for holding me always in the palm of Your hands. I pray today that I will use my hands for good: to help a child, to give a hug, to pat a back, to cook a meal, to touch with kindness, to caress with love. I lift up my hands to praise You and fold them in prayer to intercede. In Jesus' name, amen.

ADDITIONAL SCRIPTURE READING: PROVERBS 31:10-31

Breaking the Will but Not the Spirit

Submit yourselves, then, to God.

JAMES 4:7

Of all of the activities ten-year-old Miriam enjoyed, she loved riding her horse, Charlie, the best. He had a sleek chestnut mane, well-defined muscular legs, and a fierce strong will to match. Miriam felt powerful and self-assured when controlling this massive animal—except when he caught a glimpse of the barn. Whenever Miriam and Charlie returned from a jaunt in the woods, as soon as they got close enough for him to see the barn, he bolted homeward, forcing Miriam to hang on to the reins for dear life.

One day Miriam's riding instructor witnessed this strong-willed animal taking control of his master.

"Miriam!" she called out. "You cannot let that animal control you in that manner! Bring that horse back out of the barn this instant."

Dutifully, Miriam mounted Charlie and led him a distance away from the stalls.

"Now, when you turn around and Charlie sees the barn and begins to run toward it," the wiser, older woman instructed, "pull the reins all the way to the right. Do not let him go forward."

On cue, Miriam steered her horse toward the stalls. On cue, he bolted.

"Turn him! Turn him!" the instructor shouted.

Young Miriam pulled the reins to the right as hard as she could until the horse's head was inches away from touching his right shoulder. Charlie fought her with the force of a war horse. Round and round the horse and rider circled.

"Don't let go," the instructor shouted. "You must break his will!"

After ten long minutes, Charlie stopped circling, and Miriam stopped pulling him to the right. Miriam gently tapped his flanks, and he slowly walked toward the stable. She had broken his will, and he now obeyed his master's touch.

Have you ever felt that you are going in circles? Perhaps God is trying to break some old habit patterns in your life to help you become more adept at sensing His gentle nudges and tender tugging. Perhaps He is trying to steer you in a different direction other than bolting to the familiar. It's an amazing ride when you yield your will to the Master and travel the path He leads.

Dear Lord, so many times I see myself in Miriam's horse. I bolt to what is familiar rather than submit to You. Help me to follow Your lead, submit to Your guidance, and walk at the pace You set. In Jesus' name, amen.

ADDITIONAL SCRIPTURE READING: JAMES 4:1-12

A Courageous Queen

Praise be to the God and Father of our Lord Jesus Christ,
the Father of compassion and the God of all comfort,
who comforts us in our troubles, so that we can comfort those
in any trouble with the comfort we
ourselves have received from God.

2 CORINTHIANS 1:3-4

Katie was born in Wichita, Kansas, a petite blond-headed pride and joy to the Signaigo family. In the following years, two more baby girls were born, and the Signaigo quiver was full. Katie grew up enjoying all the frills and thrills of childhood. She loved school and church activities, swimming and running, and most of all, she loved her friends.

Katie was only nine years old when she noticed a lump by her left ankle that wouldn't go away. The soreness would come and go, but the lump remained. For more than a year she and her mom were in and out of doctors' offices trying to figure out what this mysterious lump was all about. Two years later, eleven-year-old Katie was diagnosed with cancer, and her leg was removed just below the knee. She felt as though her life was over.

"No one will ever love me or want to marry me!" young Katie cried to her mom. "My life will never be the same. What am I going to do? People will laugh at me and make fun of me. I'll never be able to walk or run again. I'm going to have to live the rest of my life in a wheelchair!"

"Oh, precious," her mother spoke in assuring tones. "You will get married one day. You are a beautiful girl. You will run and swim and do all the things you've always loved doing. You are not going to be in a wheelchair but have a prosthetic leg that will allow you to do all the things you did before. No, your life will not be the same, but it will be great. You'll see. We'll get through this together."

As a precaution, Katie went through chemotherapy for one year.

Besides losing her leg, Katie also lost all of her beautiful blond hair. "When is this ever going to end?" she cried.

Eventually, Katie's hair grew back, she learned to walk with a prosthesis, and life returned to a new kind of normal. However, no one—absolutely no one but her immediate family—saw Katie's leg. She kept her prosthesis hidden from the world.

But then God began nudging Katie to return to the hospital where she had her surgery to talk to other children facing similar ordeals. She put her fears aside and visited the cancer ward and showed her leg to a girl named Amanda.

"Here, go ahead and touch it," Katie said. "It's okay." And Katie saw something flicker in Amanda's eyes. It was hope.

Since that time Katie and her mom have made many visits to the hospital, telling children and their parents about what to expect and sharing hope. Together they are taking their scars, both physical and emotional, and investing them in others.

Katie graduated from high school and attended the University of Central Arkansas. While there, she watched an *Oprah* program that featured Aimee Mullins, a double amputee who had become an athlete and a model. This amputee even showed various prostheses she used for different occasions.

So Katie decided it was time to stop hiding her leg from the world, and she did it in a big way. She entered the Miss University of Central Arkansas pageant! She participated in the talent, evening gown, and interview competitions. But Katie won the hearts of the crowd when she proudly walked down the catwalk in the bathing suit competition. There have been many tearful moments as pageant sponsors have placed the crowns on a winner's head, but I dare say there was never a more precious moment than when Katie Signaigo was crowned Miss UCA.

"We are all cracked pots in some way or other," Katie told a group of ladies at a women's gathering. "We all have our unique flaws. Don't be afraid of your flaws. Look for the positive things in life. Don't let yourself dwell in the bad things. This has been the greatest blessing in my life."

Like with Katie, often God uses our biggest struggles as a springboard for ministry. Listen closely. Is God calling you to use what you've gone through to encourage others with the hope and healing of Jesus Christ?

Dear Lord, sometimes I get stuck when life doesn't turn out the way I thought it would. Help me to be a woman who refuses to say, "Why me?" but rejoices in saying "What now?" Show me how to turn my pain into purpose and my miseries into ministry. In Jesus' name, amen.

ADDITIONAL SCRIPTURE READING: 2 CORINTHIANS 1:3-11

Grandma's Inheritance

Older women...encourage the young women to love their husbands,
to love their children, to be sensible, pure, workers at home.

TITUS 2:3-5 NASB

As far as I can remember, my Grandma Edwards was always old. She didn't have many material possessions, but she had a sharp mind, a determined spirit, and buckets full of love. She was a small-framed woman who raised a family of five children during the Depression by running a country general store and harvesting produce from her garden. Her waist-long, tightly braided hair wound around her head like a crown, and her teeth came out at night.

Another thing that always amazed me as a little girl was Grandma's undergarments. She wore knit baggy underwear that hung down to her knees and an equally attractive T-shirt to match. I never saw these undergarments anywhere except on Grandma's clothesline, so I decided there must be a special "Grandma store" that sold baggy underwear just for grandparents.

Grandma never drove a car, but she would ring up the grocery store and a box of supplies would magically appear on her back stoop. Grandma's house was filled with the aroma of strong coffee and fresh-baked biscuits. There was also the scent of salve, which was the cure-all for any ailment, and of snuff, which she would sneak between her cheek and gum when she thought I wasn't looking.

Each summer I would spend a week at Grandma's house. The highlight of our day was watching Perry Mason on her big black-and-white television. We drank Coca-Cola from cold glass bottles and ate peanut butter crackers. Grandma had a standing date with Perry each day. If someone "came a'callin'" during that time, they knew to pull up a chair, grab a Coke, and wait until the verdict was in before conversation could commence.

During my weeks with Grandma, there were no trips to fast-food

restaurants or shopping sprees at the mall. That's just not what grandmas were for. So what did I do for seven days? I did what Grandma did
(except dip snuff). I made biscuits, shelled lima beans, canned vegeta-
bles for the following winter, and learned how to sew.

When I was six years old, Grandma taught me how to turn a square
piece of daisy-covered fabric into a gathered apron with a big bow in
the back. At seven, we transformed a rectangular piece of floral cloth
into a jumper with big ball buttons on the straps. At eight, we con-
quered the zipper.

Without realizing it, my grandmother was being a Titus 2 woman.
"Older women…encourage the young women to love their husbands,
to love their children, to be sensible, pure, workers at home." It was
her inheritance to me.

Grandma didn't leave me a sum of money when she passed away,
but she left something much more valuable. God used her to show
me that leaving an inheritance to our children is so much more than
money in the bank, well-invested mutual funds, and valuable heirlooms. It is leaving them memories of simple times together, showing
them how to become men and women of God, and leaving a legacy
that causes them to "rise up and call you blessed."

What sort of legacy will you leave behind? The more we become
women who listen to God, the more likely we will leave a yearning in
others to do the same.

Dear Lord, help me to leave a godly heritage and invest
love today that will multiply tomorrow. Help me to always
remember what is important—not money in the bank,
but God in the heart. Help me to be the type of woman
that we read about in Titus 2. In Jesus' name, amen.

ADDITIONAL SCRIPTURE READING: LUKE 1:36-45,56

The Hidden Key

*When I kept silent, my bones wasted away through my
groaning all day long. For day and night your hand was
heavy upon me; my strength was sapped as in the heat of
summer. Then I acknowledged my sin to you and did not
cover up my iniquity. I said, "I will confess my transgressions
to the LORD"—and you forgave the guilt of my sin.*

PSALM 32:3

When I was a teenager, my high school was just a few miles from my home. My lunch break was a mere 35 minutes, but I enjoyed driving home and taking a respite from the hustle and bustle of the crowded hallways.

Rocky Mount, North Carolina, was a sleepy little town with a railroad track that ran down the middle of downtown, dividing it into two counties. There was a fledgling minor league baseball team that ranked in *Sports Illustrated* as the worst housing conditions in the league, and a Hardee's fast-food restaurant on every corner, reminding us that the corporate office for the chain was just down the street. We slept with our windows open, left home with our doors unlocked, and as children we rode our bicycles all over town without a hint of reservation.

But times changed in the late sixties and early seventies. We began to keep our windows closed at night and our doors locked even during the day. Kids stayed much closer to home. At our house, we kept an extra key in the mailbox just inside the doorless garage. The only people who knew it was there were our family and the mailman...or so we thought.

During my high school years when I went home for lunch at 12:10 every day, I simply retrieved the key from the mailbox and then placed it back until I came home again at 3:15.

One day I came home after school at the usual time, used the hidden key, and let myself in. Before grabbing a snack, I made a bee-line to the television to turn on my favorite program. When I opened the door, I realized the TV was missing.

I didn't know anything was wrong with the TV, I thought. *Mom must have taken it into the shop for repairs.*

I called Mom at her craft store.

"Hello, Bee N' Beetle. May I help you?"

"Hey, Mom. This is Sharon. Did you take the TV in for repair?"

"No, I didn't. Why?"

"Well, because it isn't here."

"What do you mean, it isn't there?"

"It's not here. The cabinet is empty."

"Is anything else missing?" she asked with a hint of fear in her voice.

"I don't know. Let me check."

I didn't have to look far to see that a few other items were gone. When I came back to the phone to report, my mother said, "Sharon, quick! Get out of there!"

When the police came, we discovered that someone had indeed broken into our house and taken many things. And how did he get in? Why, he used the hidden key!

Apparently, someone had been watching me. He knew I came home at 12:10 and left again at 12:45. He also knew I came home from school around 3:15. So between 12:45 and 3:15, he simply took the key from the mailbox, let himself in, and helped himself to our belongings. Then, when he had what he wanted, the thief locked the door behind him and put the key back in the mailbox for "safekeeping."

That's exactly what Satan does in our lives. He watches us and knows exactly where that hidden key to our secret places lies. Then, at the most opportune times, he unlocks the door to steal our peace and joy. The Bible tells us that Satan is a roaring lion seeking someone to devour (1 Peter 5:8). Sometimes the hidden parts of our hearts, the ones that we have not given to God, are where Satan wants to sink his teeth. As long as we have that key hidden, Satan can get to it.

There's only one solution: Don't hide the key. Give the key to every compartment of your heart to God.

Listen closely. Is God prompting you to give Him the key to a hidden room in your heart today?

Dear Lord, I give You the key to my heart—my whole heart. I give You the key to every secret closet, every hidden room, every messy nook and cranny of my life. No longer will I keep those keys to myself but hand them over to You totally and completely to do with what You will. In Jesus' name, amen.

ADDITIONAL SCRIPTURE READING: PSALM 32:1-11

Adopted

In love he predestined us to be adopted as his sons
through Jesus Christ, in accordance with his pleasure and will.

EPHESIANS 1:4-5

Debbie took her 13-year-old son, Jason, to the dermatologist to have a few suspicious moles examined. The doctor asked her, "Has anyone on your or your husband's side of the family had melanoma or any other types of skin cancer?"

"No, I can't think of any," she replied.

The doctor asked a few other questions about their family history and then wrapped up the exam.

When he left the room, Jason looked up at Debbie and said, "Mom, when the doctor asked about your family history, it didn't matter. I'm adopted!"

"You're right, Jason. I totally forgot."

Debbie had gone through five years of infertility treatments and two years waiting to adopt a child. Eight months after she adopted Jason, she found out she was pregnant with Jordan. Amazingly, these boys looked almost like twins for much of their lives.

At that moment Debbie had totally forgotten he was adopted. He was simply her son, period. Ephesians 1:5 says we have been adopted as sons [and daughters] through Jesus Christ. God has chosen us to be His own—adopted into His family and co-heirs with Christ.

I think that God, like Debbie, probably forgets we're adopted. He just sees us as His children. And look what we receive just by being part of the family:

- The light of Christ   Matthew 5:14
- The friendship of Christ   John 15:15
- The power of Christ   Romans 8:37

- The mind of Christ   1 Corinthians 2:16
- The fragrance of Christ   2 Corinthians 2:15

Dear Abba Father, how precious that we get to call You "Daddy." Thank You for choosing me to be Your child. I am so grateful that I belong to a big, loving family of believers, and I can't wait until we have our family reunion in eternity with You. In Jesus' name, amen.

ADDITIONAL SCRIPTURE READING: EPHESIANS 1:1-14

Put a Lid on It

The tongue is a small part of the body, but it makes great boasts.
Consider what a great forest is set on fire by a small spark.

JAMES 3:5

From the time I could hold a crayon in my chubby little hand, I've enjoyed creating various works of art. For my family and friends, my annual endeavors usually found their way under the Christmas tree and into their hands. One year it was macramé hanging plant holders woven with wooden beads. Another it was a menagerie of decoupage wooden boxes. Then there were the years of framed cross-stitch, ceramic Nativity sets, and quilted pig and chicken pillows.

When I was 17, it was the year of the candle. Everyone from Grandma Edwards to my best girlfriends received praying hands candles. For weeks I slaved over a hot stove, stirring melted wax, meticulously centering the ten-inch wicks, and then slowly pouring the red, green, or yellow molten material into an inverted mold in the shape of praying hands. When the wax hardened, I burped the rubber mold and plopped the hands onto the counter. My kitchen looked like a prostheses laboratory with hands littering the counters.

I was just cooking up my last batch of wax when the doorbell rang. I was having so much fun that I had forgotten the time. I had a date at 7:30, and here I was in pink curlers and a paraffin-covered sweatshirt. I rushed through the kitchen, leaped over my dad, who had fallen asleep on the den floor in front of the television, and threw open the door.

"Hi, Jim. Come on in," I said, out of breath. "I'm not ready."

"So I noticed," he said with a grin.

"I was cooking candles and lost track of time."

"You were what?"

"Oh, never mind. Just come on in and have a seat on the couch. I'll be ready in a minute."

I dashed to my room to change clothes, take out the curlers and run a brush through my hair, swipe mascara through my lashes, and place a hint of gloss on my lips. Jim sat uncomfortably on the sofa, listening to my dad snore and Jackie Gleason yell at Ralph Kramden. After about 15 minutes Jim smelled something burning from the kitchen. He didn't want to call me for fear of waking up my dad. (Teenage boys don't like to wake up their date's dad if they can help it.) Instead, he tiptoed into the kitchen and discovered a pot on the stove with flames shooting up about 18 inches in the air.

Sleeping dad or no sleeping dad, Jim yelled, "Sharon! Whatever you were cooking is on fire!"

"Oh my goodness!" I exclaimed. "I forgot to turn off the stove!"

Just as I burst into the kitchen, Jim threw a cup of water into the flaming wax. Rather than extinguish the flames, the fire exploded upward. The flames shot up the wall, across the ceiling, and down the other side of the room. Our screams alerted my father, who woke to see us standing in a room surrounded by flames. With the agility of Superman, Dad sprang to his feet, ran to the kitchen faster than a speeding bullet, grabbed the lid of the pot, and clamped it down on the source of the flames. Just as quickly as the fire had erupted, it seemed to recede back into the pot like a genie returning to his bottle.

This all happened in a matter of seconds. We stood in the middle of the room like three stunned deer. I never did tell my dad that it was Jim who threw the water on the burning wax. Teenage boys have two strikes against them just by walking through the doors to pick up a man's baby girl.

After the shock of the incident wore off, I had time to reflect on the speed at which the flames blazed around the room, the feeling of fire licking against my skin, the terrifying sound of the fire. It made me think about my words and how easily they can explode and singe those around me. I saw and understood the destructive power of our words and the speed at which that destruction can spread. But you know what else I learned? I learned just how easy it is to stop the blaze…put a lid on it. As soon as my father placed a lid on the pot and removed the flames' source of oxygen, the fire went out.

As we listen to God day by day, I pray we will sense His leading to put a lid on our destructive words. Let's pray we will be quick to listen, slow to speak, and quick to obey when God warns us to keep fire-sparking words from slipping past our lips.

Dear Lord, set a guard over my mouth. Keep watch over the door of my lips. May nothing escape my mouth today that is not pleasing to You. In Jesus' name, amen.

ADDITIONAL SCRIPTURE READING: JAMES 3:1-18

The Interview

*Believe in the Lord Jesus, and you will be
saved—you and your household.*

ACTS 16:31

My palms were sweaty, yet my hands were still. My posture was poised, yet not stiff. My dress was conservative, yet fashionable. I waited in a small room lined with bookshelves, diplomas, and awards. A mammoth wooden desk dwarfed my small chair positioned in the center of the interrogation room.

It was the day of my first job interview. After completing dental hygiene school and passing both state and national boards, I was ready to cross over the bridge to the land of the employed. Even though Dr. Ford (the man who would decide my professional destiny) seemed somewhat intimidating, I felt fairly confident. My GPA was excellent and board scores commendable. I was ready for anything this guy had to throw at me. *Let the games begin,* I mused. And so they did.

"What was the last book you read?" Dr. Ford asked.

"*Reviewing for National Boards* and *The Four Loves* by C.S. Lewis," I replied.

"What did you eat for breakfast this morning?"

"Sarah Lee coffee cake and milk."

"What's your least favorite household job?"

"Dusting."

"What would you do if you bought a set of living room furniture and it went on sale the next day?"

"Return it and buy it back again at the sale price."

This line of rapid-fire questioning went on for 45 minutes. For each question, I shot back an honest response. But all the while I was thinking, *What does any of this have to do with dentistry? Is this what I've studied so hard for?*

After a few more minutes of chitchat, Dr. Ford leaned forward, and with a smile he said, "Sharon, we would like for you to join our team."

I was shocked! In my naïveté, I looked my prospective boss in the eye and asked, "Aren't you even going to ask me what kind of grades I made in school?"

With that Dr. Ford threw back his head and filled the room with thunderous laughter. "I imagine they were pretty good," he answered with a twinkle in his eye.

I could feel the color start at the end of my toes and rise to the top of my head. How did that question escape my lips? I couldn't believe I had said that out loud. I wanted to crawl under my chair and never come out.

Thus began my career in dentistry. I learned a lot over the next few years, but perhaps the most important lesson took place in the interview. What I discovered was that Dr. Ford was much more interested in my character than my credentials, and what was in my heart rather than in my head.

I imagine when we have our very last interview, that moment when we approach the gates of heaven, God won't ask how well we've performed on earth. He won't care about our trophies or ribbons of achievement. Like my first interview so long ago, God won't be as concerned with what's in our heads but what's in our hearts.

"Do you confess with your mouth Jesus as Lord and believe in your heart that I raised Him from the dead?" He'll ask.

What would be your answer to Him today? It will determine your eternal destiny.

⌒

Dear God, I know You are not impressed with worldly accomplishments but with holy hearts. Thank You for giving me the assurance of salvation through Jesus Christ. When that last interview takes place as I cross from this life to the next, I'll be ready. In Jesus' name, amen.

ADDITIONAL SCRIPTURE READING: ACTS 16:16-31

Refinished and Restored

If anyone is in Christ, he is a new creation;
the old has gone, the new has come!

2 CORINTHIANS 5:17

Junk. That's what my family and friends thought of most of my purchases. But to me, they were treasures waiting to be revealed.

When I was in my late teens, I had an unusual fetish for beat-up antique furniture. While most of my friends were at the mall shopping for clothes, I was at estate sales, flea markets, yard sales, and auctions hunting for antiques. Often, when I brought my purchases home, my family would roll their eyes and say, "I can't believe you paid money for that old piece of junk." But I never saw my purchases as junk. They just needed a little work...okay, sometimes a lot of work.

At one estate sale I spied a little drop leaf kitchen table with three spindle-back chairs. I could just imagine a sweet little older lady spending many years sitting at that very table drinking her morning coffee or perhaps her afternoon tea. I could almost hear the faint whispers of thousands of conversations from generations past. The set was painted a hospital green, but I saw that it had great potential. Obviously the other bidders didn't recognize a treasure when they saw one, because ten minutes and $35 later, the set was mine.

I brought the dinette set home, all excited about my great buy, and couldn't understand why no one else shared my enthusiasm.

"Sharon, do you realize how much time and energy it is going to take to make that old green rickety table look even slightly presentable?" they asked. At that point in my life, I had a lot more time than money, so the time wasn't a problem.

Refinishing furniture is a dirty, grueling task. First, I stripped off the paint with paint remover and discovered that not only had the table been green, it had also been blue, and before that white. But underneath it all was pure walnut.

The paint remover raised the grain of the wood, so I had to go back and sand it smooth. If the sanding isn't done well, the finished product will always be a little rough. A few joints were loose from wear and tear, so I glued them back together. Then I applied a warm walnut stain which deepened its color and made the beautiful pattern of the wood grain stand out. Finally, I applied a polyurethane coat to seal and protect the piece.

As I worked I began to think of the old broken table as a symbol of my own life. I was also on the auction block, and God purchased me with His Son's precious blood. I had layers and layers of my old self that had to be stripped away to reveal the beauty hidden beneath. This raised my grain, but God sanded me with life experiences and trials to remove the rough edges. He glued my loose joints and mended my broken pieces, for He heals the brokenhearted and binds up their wounds. Then He put a sealer not only on me but in me—the Holy Spirit—who brought out the beauty of who God created me to be.

After I finished refurbishing the old table and chairs, I sat in the garage thinking about all that God had done in my life. My mom opened the door, looked at the old table, and said, "I never thought something so ugly could turn out to be so beautiful."

I said, "Amen."

Where are you in the refinishing process? It's never really over, this side of heaven. But as we listen to God day by day, He will show us what needs to be stripped off, sanded away, and polished smooth to be all that He has created us to be.

Dear Lord, I was such a mess before You transformed me. Thank You for restoring my soul, renewing my spirit, and redeeming my life to become Your treasured possession…a true work of art. In Jesus' name, amen.

ADDITIONAL SCRIPTURE READING: 2 CORINTHIANS 5:1-21

No Clams for Larry

Give thanks to the LORD, for he is good; his love endures forever.
1 CHRONICLES 16:34

Sometimes we like what life serves us up—and sometimes we don't. But most of the time it simply depends on the attitude of the person holding the spoon. Such was the case one evening when I went to dinner with friends to the Sanitary Fish Market. I know that is a strange name for a seafood restaurant, but it was a great place that everyone frequented in Atlantic Beach, North Carolina. Because the food was good, I guess it was an added perk to know that it was sanitary as well.

When I was 18, I had dinner at the Sanitary with some friends. Three of us were Christians and usually took a moment to ask a blessing before we ate a meal, but we had not eaten in a restaurant with Larry before. Larry was a macho man who claimed to be in control of his own destiny. He didn't need God. So when we bowed our heads to pray, Larry held his head high as if to say, "I might be at the same table with these people, but I'm not one of them."

We all ordered clam chowder as an appetizer. We had the same waitress and same chowder from the same pot. We three Holy Rollers (the name we acquired because of a ten-second prayer) dipped our spoons into our bowls and tasted chowder full of tender clams and steamy potatoes.

Then proud Larry dipped in his spoon to retrieve only broth. "Why is your chowder full of clams and potatoes," he demanded, "and all I have is broth?"

Larry was about to call the waitress over to complain when I looked up and said, "Well, maybe it's because we asked God to bless ours and you didn't."

Larry didn't complain to the fine people at the Sanitary but ate crow instead.

Just as we listen to God day by day, He is listening to us. And nothing warms His heart like a grateful and thankful heart. What is He hearing from you today?

⌒

Dear Heavenly Father, thank You...for everything!
Help me to always have a grateful heart that never
ceases to be amazed and awed at Your protection
and provision in my life. In Jesus' name, amen.

ADDITIONAL SCRIPTURE READING: 1 CHRONICLES 16:17-36

14

Good Medicine

He sent forth his word and healed them.

PSALM 107:20

In 1974 I traveled to Europe with a group of students to study abroad. My family was falling apart, and yet I felt compelled to leave the safety of my friends to spend 12 weeks with strangers. A big part of me did not want to go. Being a new Christian, I depended on my friends to keep me afloat. However, God was trying to teach me how to swim on my own.

Before I left, my group of Christian girlfriends gave me a gift. They had taken a large medicine bottle and filled it with a homemade remedy. A handwritten label was taped to the outside with the following instructions:

> For: Miss Sharon Edwards
>
> PBP 71240
>
> Take as needed for uplifting of the spirit.
>
> May be followed by faith and prayer for faster relief.
>
> Vitamin PTLa
>
> Filled by SIC

Inside the medicine bottle were 100 Bible verses written on small strips of paper and rolled up like tiny scrolls. These verses were my medicine, the pharmacists were my Sisters in Christ, and the vitamins were Praise the Lord Anyway brand.

In Mark 1:32-34, we are told that people brought many who were sick to Jesus, and He healed various diseases. Matthew Henry describes Jesus' words as a "*panpharmacon*—a salve for every sore." Don't you just love that? That's what my teenage girlfriends in God (GiGs) gave to me. They gave me God's Word, a *panpharmacon,* to take with me on my trip. He was the Great Physician, His Word was the medicine, and my GiGs were the pharmacists who fulfilled the prescription.

That gift of the heart was given to me more than 30 years ago, and yet I've carried it with me through high school, college, marriage and many, many moves. I have kept that bottle of love with me at each crossroad and bend in the road. That's the power of a woman's words to her friends. We never know how a small act of kindness will touch someone's heart for many years to come. We never know how offering just the right verse from the Bible at the right moment can heal an ailing soul.

As you listen to God today, let's ask Him if there is a particular verse He wants you to share with a friend.

Dear Heavenly Father, I thank You for my girlfriends in God that You have sent into my life at various stages and seasons. I pray I will be the kind of friend who can share the healing words in Your Holy Word when I see a hurting soul. In Jesus' name, amen.

ADDITIONAL SCRIPTURE READING: PSALM 17:1-15

Buddy Breathing

All Scripture is God-breathed.

2 TIMOTHY 3:16

L et's go scuba diving!" a friend exclaimed one hot summer day.
"That sounds great," I said. "But I don't know how."

"Just leave it to me," he said.

I was 17 when I decided to go scuba diving with some friends. I had no training and should not have been in deep water, but I was young and threw caution to the wind. The friend who took me below the surface of the deep strapped an oxygen tank on his back, a mask on his face, and flippers on his feet. I only had a mask and flippers.

"Where's my oxygen?" I asked.

"I have it," he answered as he patted the tank on his back. "What we're going to do is jump into the water together. I'm going to take a breath through the mouthpiece and then pass it to you. You'll take a breath and pass it back to me. It's called buddy breathing."

So into the ocean we jumped. He put his arm around my waist like I was a sack of potatoes and down we went. John drew oxygen from the tank and then passed the breathing apparatus to me. We took turns breathing. It then occurred to me that I was totally dependent on this young friend to keep me alive.

This was not a very smart idea, but it did leave me with a great life lesson. At various times we will all find ourselves in deep waters. We may feel as though we are drowning with no help in sight. And then a friend comes along and hands us the breathing apparatus. We take a breath and rise quickly to the surface.

Words of my friends have been like oxygen when I've felt as though I were drowning. Even today I have a mental scrapbook of encouraging words passed along to me in the ocean of despair. God has sent friends my way who have strapped on the Word of God and passed the life-giving words to me when I've needed them most.

Buddy breathing. That's what we can do for each other when a friend forgets how to draw in the air she needs. That's what God does for us each time we open the pages of His Word and listen to Him.

～

Lord, thank You for friends who breathe life into me when I feel as though I can't go on. Show me someone who needs a tender touch, a winning word, or a strong shoulder to lean on today. And, Lord, thank You for being that friend for me. In Jesus' name, amen.

ADDITIONAL SCRIPTURE READING: 2 TIMOTHY 3:1-17

Butterflies

We, who with unveiled faces all reflect the Lord's glory,
are being transformed into his likeness with ever-increasing glory,
which comes from the Lord, who is the Spirit.

2 CORINTHIANS 3:18

She flits and flutters her wings like a flirting young damsel batting feathery eyelashes at a suitor. Her yellow wings, jeweled with black and hints of red, and delicate tiny feet dance on pink and purple bouquets. A gust of wind lifts her body, and she seems to float in search of something unseen. Returning to her mission, she skims the surface of several blossoms until she finds one that pleases her. Then daintily she lights on a violet bloom and sips from it.

I love to watch butterflies drink from the flowers in my backyard. It never ceases to amaze me that this beautiful creature is birthed from an ugly brown cocoon. Yes, she is held captive for a time, but that time is not for naught. During her time in the darkness, God is shaping and molding her into a beautiful creation. Then there is a struggle for the butterfly. She must fight for days for freedom, but that fight makes her strong and prepares her for flight.

Like a butterfly, I was once held captive in a deep, dark chrysalis of fear, but the time was not for naught. God was shaping and molding me into a beautiful, colorful creature. Like the caterpillar undergoing a momentous change in the confining chrysalis, I had to go through a difficult healing process to be free of hurts from the past. I had to struggle for years, but God used the trials to transform and strengthen me to have the stamina to take flight and soar.

For my fortieth birthday, my mother gave me a beautiful butterfly necklace. The right wing of the butterfly was crafted from my father's wedding band, which had been melted down, and the left wing from hers. In the middle sparkled the diamond from her engagement ring.

Each time I wear the necklace, I am reminded of the necessity of the cocoon years in my own life and the beauty of the end result.

The chrysalis years are necessary for developing strength and character to fly. And what a joy to soar to heights unimaginable by the breath of the Savior, who makes all things beautiful in His time.

Friend, if you are in the chrysalis years, don't give up. Soon it will be time to soar! If you are already flying in freedom, thank God for seeing you through.

Dear God, thank You for the dark times when I struggled with life. I know that the lessons learned in the dark have given me spiritual strength and beauty to soar with confidence today. In Jesus' name, amen.

ADDITIONAL SCRIPTURE READING: 2 CORINTHIAN 3:7-18

Grafted On

Branches were broken off so that I could be grafted in.

ROMANS 11:19

Julianna came out of the womb ready to meet every challenge with determination, every celebration with enthusiasm, and every mystery with the passion of discovery. Her fiery red hair matched her fiery personality. She never did anything halfway, but with the throttle wide open. Of the Prices' three children, Julianna was the one who frequented the emergency room for stitches due to throwing caution to the wind as she whirled through her childhood.

At 12 years old, Julianna graced the dance floor with other aspiring ballerinas. One unforgettable Thursday, a neighbor came to pick her up for dance class. In her usual fashion, Julianna rushed out like a whirlwind and slammed the door behind her. However, the door closed before her hand made it across the threshold. Julianna jerked to a sudden halt, spun around quickly, and made a horrible discovery.

"Help! Somebody help me! I've just cut off my finger!"

Sure enough, Julianna had amputated the upper third of her middle finger on her right hand. Providentially, the woman picking her up for dance class was a nurse and knew just what to do for the screaming ballerina.

"Let's put some pressure on that nub," she said. "Daniel!" she called to Julianna's brother. "Come help us!"

Daniel, Julianna's 15-year-old brother, ran down the stairs at the cry for help. "Julianna cut off her finger," the nurse explained. "You have to find it. We have to put it in ice and take her to the hospital before it's too late."

They arrived at the hospital just in time. A skilled doctor put Humpty Dumpty back together again and told them to pray the finger would reattach.

A few days later Julianna unwrapped the bandage, afraid of what she might find underneath. What she saw was not a pretty sight. Instead of a finger, she saw a black mushroomlike thimble sitting atop her nub.

"Doctor, we took the bandage off today," her mom reported. "The finger is black and crusty and looks as though it has a mushroom cap sitting on top. It looks dead."

"That's fine," he reassured her. "Don't worry. If nature is working properly, and it sounds like it is, the top will turn black, but underneath nerves and blood vessels are reattaching. Beneath the 'thimble' a new finger is forming. She needs the old part in order for the new part to form. We'll know in about three weeks if the procedure worked. Just keep it wrapped and clean."

A couple of weeks after the accident, Julianna came to spend the night with us while she was attending a dance camp in my hometown. I had the pleasure of her company and the displeasure of changing her bandage. Her description was accurate.

Four weeks after Julianna had returned home, she wrote me a thank-you note for having her in our home. She ended by saying, "P.S. Guess what? My crusty thimble fell off and I have a new finger!"

Now, don't ask me how this transformation happened. It's a mystery to me. But Scripture tells of another grafting procedure that is even more astounding. Though we were spiritually dead, cut off and rotten to the core, God demonstrated His love for us by grafting us onto the living root, Jesus Christ, and making us alive together with Him. Now that's a miracle.

And because of that miracle, God opens our spiritual eyes to see Him and our spiritual ears to hear Him day by day.

⌒

Dear Heavenly Father, thank You for grafting me onto the living root of Jesus Christ. It is a miracle that You could take a dead spirit like mine, graft it onto the vine of Jesus Christ, and make me spiritually alive in Him. I pray my fruit will glorify You as I continue to grow in Your heavenly vineyard. In Jesus' name, amen.

ADDITIONAL SCRIPTURE READING: ROMANS 11:11-24

The Gift

The greatest of these is love.

1 CORINTHIANS 13:13

Y ou'll need that."
"That'll come in handy."
"You can never have too many mixing bowls."

Bridal showers are so predictable. Mounds of various-sized boxes wrapped in shiny silver and glossy white paper, topped with beautifully crafted bows. Toaster ovens, electric can openers, stainless steel mixing bowls, everyday dishes, and fine china. Oooh's and aaah's echo around the room from spectators as each treasure is carefully unwrapped and passed around the crowd for inspection. Comments from a choir of onlookers who have traveled this road years before fill the room.

My bridal shower was no exception. The story was the same as the thousands before mine. However, one present stood out above all the Crock-Pots, bath towels, and silverware. It was a gift from my mother.

Mom was one of 12 children raised on a tobacco farm in Nash County, North Carolina. During her fifth year of marriage, she discovered she was pregnant with her second child. To pass the time, her mother-in-law taught her how to crochet using household twine—the same twine used on their tobacco farm to tie up the amber leaves to dry. She didn't know a lot about the fine gauge of 100 percent wool skeins of yarn, but she knew about the strength and durability of 100 percent cotton twine.

During the nine months she carried me in her womb, Mom's nimble fingers crafted a beautifully crocheted bedspread. Love was woven into every stitch. The last of the fringe was tatted a few days before I made my grand debut. She tucked the bedspread away for this very day, 23 years later.

Her baby girl grew too large for her crib and was too soon ready for her first bed. But it wasn't the masterpiece her mom had created that graced her bed. Instead, ballerinas in airy white and pink tutus danced across the fabric of the spread and on the canopy overhead. The crocheted bedspread was buried away like a treasure.

At my bridal shower, ladies crowded around to see what grand finale my mom had saved as the last gift to be opened. I carefully plucked the bow from its lid, tore away the elegant wrapping, and removed the top. Gently I folded back layers of tissue paper to reveal the beautiful masterpiece Mom created while God created me.

"You can never have too many bedspreads," commented one of the old-timers.

"And you can never have too much love," I replied.

Four years later, as God was knitting together my first child in my womb, I took up quilting. My first project took eight months to complete and love was woven into each tiny stitch. I have visions of one day taking this quilt to my son's fiancée's bridal shower. Then among the gifts of pots and pans, she'll open the beautifully wrapped box.

Someone will say, "You can never have too many quilts."

And I will echo, "And you can never have too much love."

You may not be crafty with needle and thread, but with strands of love you are stitching days together into a work of art. Now, who are you going to give that to?

⌒

Heavenly Father, make me a vessel of Your love today. Show me on whom I need to pour it. And thank You that I never have to worry about running out of love, because You have an endless supply to fill me up again. In Jesus' name, amen.

ADDITIONAL SCRIPTURE READING: 1 CORINTHIANS 13:1-13

19

Make Each Moment Count

I will sing to the LORD all my life;
I will sing praise to my God as long as I live.

PSALM 104:33

What would you do today if you knew you only had a few months to live?

When I was newly married, I attended a social club meeting of women whose husbands shared the same profession. There was nothing wrong with the gathering. The food was good. Smiles were warm. Conversations were light. But I walked away feeling as though I'd wasted a precious gift—a morning of my life.

The next month I opted not to attend. Instead, I went to a nursery to pick out some flowers to plant in my garden. While musing among the impatiens and begonias, I spotted Carol, a woman whose husband was also in the same profession as mine. Two little girls followed after her as she carefully chose blue, pink, and yellow perennials that would bloom year after year. Carol had cancer and had been given only a few months to live.

Suddenly God spoke to my heart. *Sharon, if you knew you had only a few months to live, would you be at the social club meeting or buying flowers with your children? How would you spend your day?*

It was a poignant moment as I was reminded of the brevity of life. We never know how much or how little time we have on this earth. I resolved at that moment to spend each day as if it were my last...to make each day count.

Even today I think of the flowers still blooming in Carol's yard year after year. My hope and prayer is that the seeds I plant along life's journey will continue to bloom years after I'm gone.

So let's go back to my original question: What would you do today if you knew you only had a few months to live?

Dear God, thank You for the gift of this day. Help me to live today and every day as if it could be my last. Help me to make each moment count. In Jesus' name, amen.

ADDITIONAL SCRIPTURE READING: PSALM 104:1-35

20

Reflexes

Train yourself to be godly.

1 TIMOTHY 4:7

It was hot. The traffic was heavy. I was young and distracted. I was driving alone in the flow of vacationer traffic traveling to and from the North Carolina coast. I was in the group headed for home. The July traffic was bumper-to-bumper, with everyone going faster than the posted speed limit. I had other things on my mind besides maneuvering in traffic and was paying little attention to the cars around me.

Traveling 60 miles per hour in my sporty two-tone Pontiac Sunbird, I felt my front right tire slip off of the asphalt and onto the gravel shoulder of the road. In a flood of panic, I heard the voice of my driver's ed instructor from four years before, "If you run off the road, do not, and I repeat, do not jerk your car back on the road. Slow to a stop and then gently guide the car back on the road."

My mind knew the rule. I was even repeating, "Do not jerk the car. Do not jerk the car." Then I promptly jerked the car. I pulled the steering wheel to the left, jerked the car onto the road, and lost control. First the Sunbird flew across two lanes of traffic to the left and then, after overcorrecting again, she flew back off the road to the right. As if in slow motion, the car began a descent down an embankment. The weight of the car became unbalanced, and it began to roll like a toy tossed by an angry child. As the car somersaulted down the embankment, my body tossed and tumbled like a rag doll, bouncing around the car's interior. I wasn't wearing my seat belt. When the car landed upside down at the bottom of the embankment, I was sitting on the ceiling on the passenger's side.

Travelers watched aghast as the scenario played out before them. You can imagine how amazed they were to see me crawl out of the car's open window without a scratch. I knew, without a doubt, that I should not have lived through that accident. It was only by the grace of God that I survived.

Thinking back on that event, I am reminded how powerful reflexes are. When the car veered off the road, I knew what to do, but I did the opposite. I knew not to jerk the steering wheel, but I did it anyway.

Sometimes we know in our heads what we are supposed to do, but the reflexes of old programming overcome reason. The Bible tells us that when we come to Christ, we are a new creation (2 Corinthians 5:17). However, no one pushes the delete button to erase old habit patterns that have been formed over time. Only through prayer and practice can we retrain our old ways and habits to form new godly reflexes that will reflect the nature of Christ.

In the meantime, let's listen to God before we act, and retrain those old reflexes to match up with our new identity as children of God.

Dear Lord, why do I do what I don't want to do and not do what I want to do? Help me train my spiritual reflexes so that my initial reaction and response to every situation is a reflection of Your character and Your ways. In Jesus' name, amen.

ADDITIONAL SCRIPTURE READING: 1 TIMOTHY 4:7-16

21

Hush My Mouth

*Why do you look at the speck of sawdust in your brother's eye
and pay no attention to the plank in your own eye? How can
you say to your brother, "Let me take the speck out of your
eye," when all the time there is a plank in your own eye?*

MATTHEW 7:3-4

I couldn't believe it. The announcement of one of the most important days of my life…my dream come true…and there was a misprint! A horrible misprint. My husband and I were married in a small eastern North Carolina town on a beautiful August afternoon. There's not a lot going on in Rocky Mount, so weddings and funerals receive full coverage. My wedding picture, in all its bridal glory, was a 4 x 5 crisp black-and-white photo displayed in the local section of the paper. Under my smiling face read the caption…Mrs. Steven *Hush* Jaynes.

I was mortified! My mother-in-law did not have a lapse in judgment when Steve was born. She did not name him Hush. His middle name is Hugh. Oh my goodness. What were those people thinking? How could they be so careless? Didn't they realize I would cut that picture out and place it in my wedding album for all eternity? Didn't they understand the teasing that would surely follow that misprint? Didn't they understand how important this was? Hush! I was furious.

My only hope was that the even smaller town where I was actually born would also run the wedding announcement. They did. A few days after discovering the "Hush" dilemma, the tiny newspaper from Spring Hope, North Carolina, arrived. I unfolded the page and there, as big as day, was my wedding picture. This one was 5 x 7. And underneath it read…Mrs. Steven *Hush* Jaynes. Oh my glory! Now I was crying.

On the same day I received the newspaper from my husband's hometown of more than 500,000 people. Underneath my itty-bitty wedding picture were the words…you guessed it…Mrs. Steven *Hush* Jaynes!

Suddenly the truth began to sink in. This was not the error of inept newspapers. It was my fault. When I print, I'm a bit sloppy, and my *g* seldom closes, looking like an *s*. I guess it looks a lot like an *s*. So now it was time for me to hush.

Have you ever been in a situation where you were blaming someone for a mishap and suddenly realized you were the one at fault? Jesus said it this way, "Why do you look at the speck of sawdust in your brother's eye and pay no attention to the plank in your own eye? How can you say to your brother, 'Let me take the speck out of your eye,' when all the time there is a plank in your own eye?" (Matthew 7:3-4).

I have since learned that when you point a finger at someone, there are at least three other fingers pointing back at yourself. The best way to avoid that is not to point the finger at someone in the first place.

Jesus went on to say, "First take the plank out of your own eye, and then you will see clearly to remove the speck from your brother's eye" (Matthew 7:5). I don't know about you, but I have plenty of sawdust in my own life to keep me busy without worrying about what's in someone else's.

I still put the newspaper announcements in our wedding album. It is a great reminder of two truths. Number one: August 16, 1980, was one of the happiest days of my life. Number two: Before I start casting blame or pointing fingers, I need to take a good look in the mirror and hush.

How are you in the finger-pointing department? Here's an idea. When feeling the urge to point a finger and place blame on someone, fold your hands together and pray instead. What God reveals might be surprising.

Dear Heavenly Father, sometimes I am too quick to blame someone else for my mistakes. Help me to always examine my own heart and let You take care of the rest. Thank You for the embarrassing reminders that I am a work in progress and You are not finished with me yet. In Jesus' name, amen.

ADDITIONAL SCRIPTURE READING: MATTHEW 7:1-6

22

Restoring Someone's Broken Dream

"I know the plans I have for you," declares the LORD,
*"plans to prosper you and not to harm you, plans
to give you hope and a future."*

JEREMIAH 29:11

I live about 200 miles from the coast. And yet our local Walmart has a random smattering of seagulls that soar overhead and eat french fries and other debris from neighboring fast-food restaurants. The truth is, the seagulls are lost. They have taken a wrong turn. And instead of discovering where they went wrong, they have settled for the asphalt parking lot rather than the salty sea. They have reconciled themselves to feeding on the refuge and trash of harried shoppers rather than the fresh seafood cuisine of their feathered forefathers.

And you know what? It's not just the seagulls who are lost...who have forgotten the reason for their very existence, the habitat for which they were created to survive and thrive. It is human beings as well. Many have become lost. They are standing in the parking lot of life subsisting off of the refuse of fast living.

Someone needs to point them to the ocean of opportunity, the sea of success, the shore of satisfaction. And I'm not talking about money or materialism...those things that *are* mere french fries compared to the abundant life that God has for His image bearers. "'For I know the plans I have for you,' declares the LORD, 'plans to prosper you and not to harm you, plans to give you hope and a future'" (Jeremiah 29:11).

Do you know someone who is discouraged? Who has taken a wrong turn in life? Who has let the fire go out on their hopes and dreams? A friend? A husband? A child? If so, you could become the encourager who fans a small spark of potential into a flame.

And maybe you are that person who has forgotten her dreams. Who has lost her way. Listen closely to what God has to say to you:

"No eye has seen, no ear has heard, no mind has conceived what I [God] have prepared for those who love Me" (1 Corinthians 2:9). And that includes you!

Dear Father, all around me I see people who have settled for less than Your best. They have given up on their hopes and dreams. But, Lord, I don't want to be one of those people. Are there dreams in my own life I have forgotten? Have I settled for less than Your best? If I have, please reveal that to me and give me the courage to get out of the parking lot of life and soar to the places You had planned all along. In Jesus' name, amen.

ADDITIONAL SCRIPTURE READING: JEREMIAH 29:11-14

23

Just What You've Always Wanted

I came so they can have real and eternal life,
more and better life than they ever dreamed of.

JOHN 10:10 MSG

Yard sales. I've never really liked them. But when we were preparing to move from the home we had lived in for 20 years, we decided it was a must. It was a way to clean out the clutter, make a little money, and not haul yesterday's treasures to today's trash.

We displayed our lovely attic decor on makeshift plywood tables and waited for the bargain babes to descend. We were not disappointed. Two hours before the advertised opening time, treasure hunters began congregating outside the closed garage doors. Then, upon the unveiling, the swarm attacked.

Among the valuables from my past sat an electric ceramic Christmas tree with various colored lights...no doubt a gift from the eighties. One particular woman perused the lovely display and came upon this "magnificent work of art."

"I've always wanted one of these!" she declared with excitement in her voice. "How much is it?"

"Three dollars," my husband answered.

"Humph," she grunted and walked on.

Steve and I just looked at each other and stifled our laughter.

Let's rewind the scene for a moment. This woman said she had always wanted a ceramic Christmas tree just like that one. (I'm not here to judge another person's dreams. That's just what she said.) Always. Her whole life. And here it was! For a mere three dollars, her dream could have come true! The search over! Most likely we would have sacrificed this masterpiece for two dollars, but she didn't even ask. She just shrugged and walked away.

Then my mind began to wander through a rummage sale of its own.

I thought about the Pharisees in the Bible. For years they waited for the coming of the promised Messiah. Prayed about it. Preached about it. Prepared for it. Then, when Jesus showed up, they turned their backs and walked away. "Humph," they said with a shrug. "No thanks."

And then I thought about me...and you. How many times do *we* long for a particular dream to come true in our lives? Long for it. Search for it. Obsess over it. A husband. A child. A job. A home. Then one day, there it is! It can be ours! The search is over! We say our "I do's," bring home the bundle of joy, log in our first eight hours, hang the last curtain. But then a little time passes. The husband is not as romantic as we had hoped, the kids are not as obedient and loving as we had imagined, the job isn't as rewarding as we had envisioned, and the house is a never-ending maze of maintenance. "Humph," we grumble. We think we want something, and then when we get it, we decide we really don't want it after all.

Let me take it one step further. How many times do we long for love, joy, and peace in our lives? We search for it, long for it, and pray about it. Then someone points us to the cross and says, "There it is. It can be yours for the asking. It's not three dollars, two dollars, or even one dollar. It's free!"

"Humph," we shrug. "No thanks." And we walk away to rummage through the yard sales of life looking for treasure among other people's clutter.

Dear friend, God is holding out His holy hand with the most magnificent gift of all time—love, joy, and peace personified in His Son, Jesus Christ. He is what you have always been longing for, searching for, watching for. Jesus said, "I have come that they might have life, and have it to the full" (John 10:10). Will we take Him up on the offer or say, "Humph. No thanks," and walk away?

～

Dear Heavenly Father, thank You for making all my dreams come true. You have given me everything I have ever longed for in the person of Jesus Christ. Please forgive me for turning my back on Your amazing gift and trying to fill my longings with people and possessions. I know that nothing will ever satisfy my desire for peace, love, and joy except Jesus. In His name I pray, amen.

ADDITIONAL SCRIPTURE READING: JOHN 10:1-18

24

An Easter Bride

The wedding of the Lamb has come,
and his bride has made herself ready.

REVELATION 19:7

I t was a beautiful day for a wedding. The sun shone brightly as the daffodils danced in the gentle breeze, nodding their happy faces in conversation. A choir of robins, cardinals, and finches sang rounds of cheerful melodies, which floated through a clear blue sky that was a reflection of the bride's sparkling eyes. The air had that unusual crisp quality of spring, reminding us of the chill from winter's past and the warmth of the summer's promise.

It was Easter Sunday, the day the Groom had chosen to be joined to His beloved. He proposed to His young maiden and then promptly went away to prepare a home for her. On this day His Father signaled the home was ready, and the Son could claim His bride.

Iris had been waiting for her Husband to come and take her to the wonderful home that He had prepared for her. *How like Him to pick Easter*, she thought to herself, *my favorite day of the year.* She smiled as she heard Him coming, and her heart fluttered with the anticipation of seeing His face.

She wore a white dress with flecks of blue and carried a bouquet of pink carnations and white mums with a spray of asparagus fern as wispy as her baby-fine hair. A sweet smile spread across her face as she saw her beloved Jesus hold out His strong hand to help her across the threshold of the temporal and into the hall of eternity. She walked into His loving embrace and drank in the loveliness of her surroundings which He had perfectly described in His many letters.

On a beautiful Easter Sunday, my husband's dear, sweet, 74-year-old Aunt Iris went home to be with the Lord. As we all gathered around to say our last goodbyes, I could not manage to be mournful. Yes, I was going to miss her. But Iris had never been married on this side of eternity, and the vision I had in my mind was of her joining the Lord as the bride of Christ. For me, it was not a funeral. It was a wedding.

In Isaiah 61:3, the prophet describes what God will do for the bride of Christ. He will bestow on her a crown of beauty instead of ashes, anoint her with the oil of gladness instead of mourning, and place on her shoulders a garment of praise instead of a spirit of despair. Are you feeling brokenhearted because of your dreams of being a bride have not turned out the way you had hoped? Because perhaps your marriage is not what you had expected? God desires to blow away the ashes and place the crown of a royal bride on your head. So lift your head, dear one, and accept your crown from the King of kings.

*Dear God, thank You for choosing me to be the bride
for Your Son. Help me prepare for our wedding day
in glory by becoming a radiant woman who reflects
Your glory and grace. In Jesus' name, amen.*

ADDITIONAL SCRIPTURE READING: REVELATION 19:6-9; 21:1-21

25

Don't Let Him In

Sin is crouching at your door;
it desires to have you, but you must master it.

GENESIS 4:7

How did this happen! How am I going to get this man out of my house? Once I had a door-to-door vacuum salesman come to my home and I made a terrible mistake; I let him in. Before I could convince him I did not need a new vacuum, he had his demonstration trash sprinkled all over my foyer floor. For more than an hour the man informed me about the danger of dust mites and the benefits of his equipment.

"I already have a vacuum cleaner," I assured him.

"But not like this one, you don't!" he replied.

Finally I managed to convince this determined salesman I wasn't interested in his vacuum cleaner. He was still talking as I shoved him out the door.

"Whew! What just happened here?" I whispered as I leaned against the closed door. "Where did I go wrong?"

You let him in, God said.

Of course, God was right. My first mistake was to let him cross the threshold of my doorway and enter my home. Once he was in, it was difficult to get him out.

It is the same way with our thoughts. Once we allow the salesman (Satan) to scatter his trash in our minds, it is hard to dismiss it or push it back out again. The place of easiest victory is at the threshold. Don't even let it in the door.

It has been said that "every spiritual battle is won or lost at the threshold of the mind." I think victory is still possible once the thought has passed over the threshold, but we will save ourselves much heartache and pain if we begin to recognize Satan and what he's peddling and reject it from the start.

When a tempting thought comes knocking at the door, don't answer it. When a deceptive idea rings the bell, don't let it in. We don't want what he's selling anyway.

As we listen to God day by day, we must realize there is also an enemy who wants to sow deceptive thoughts in our minds. And the more time we spend with God, in His Word and prayer, the easier it is to detect the deceiver's voice as well.

⌐

Dear God, help me to recognize Satan's knock when
he comes tapping at the door of my mind. Give me the
wisdom and willpower to keep the door closed and not let
him in. He is not welcome here. In Jesus' name, amen.

ADDITIONAL SCRIPTURE READING: GENESIS 4:1-16

26

Potluck

There is neither Jew nor Greek, slave nor free,
male nor female, for you are all one in Christ Jesus.

GALATIANS 3:28

I recall as a young child spending time rocking on my grandma's front porch and listening to the ladies from the missions society gossip about the heathens whose church was across the street from theirs. It always puzzled me because the heathens seemed like such nice people and their church looked just like Grandma's. As far as I could tell there was no difference. Both believed in Jesus, wore funny hats on Sundays, and sang the same hymns. And both had great potluck dinners.

How did the church come up with the notion of the infamous potluck supper? As best I can tell, it all began in the fifteenth chapter of Matthew. The first gathering was a great success as Jesus served more than 4000 men, not to mention a few thousand women and children, and had leftovers to boot. All this came from one little covered dish. Actually, it was a covered basket. This was, after all, before the advent of Corningware and Tupperware.

Later the Baptists followed His lead, and the next thing you know, all denominations were celebrating a multiplicity of occasions with every variety of casserole known to man. But the twenty-first-century church isn't being caught simply serving up fish-and-chips. We have taken the notion of breaking bread and run with it. Not only do we break bread, but we crunch fried chicken, munch fresh veggies, scoop casseroles, slice pies, cut cakes, and sip coffees. We chew the fat while chewing our food and extend the right hand of fellowship while our left hand extends the serving spoon. I'd say that covered-dish dinners are one of the most cherished rituals in the church today.

One Christmas our Sunday school had a potluck dinner at the McMillians' home. Our class consisted of 150 people in a church of

1600. Because it's a little difficult to be intimate with 150 congregants on a Sunday morning, the Christmas party was a great time to chat with people you didn't normally have a chance to speak to otherwise. And because people tend to sit in the same seats each week, I'd never actually had a good look at about half of the class. The Christmas party was designed to remedy that problem.

Marshall and Denise's home was beautifully decorated with holly, spruce, and magnolia clippings. It was filled with the sights, sounds, and smells of the season as well as the incoming aroma of the many delicious prepared meals. In an effort to provide crowd control and proper traffic flow, our host, Marshall, had posted directional signs around the house. One sign read "COATS," with an arrow pointing up the stairs to their daughter's room. Another read "HOT FOOD," with an arrow pointing toward the kitchen.

Marshall was doing a great job at his post as official greeter and traffic police.

"Hello, how are you?" he said, greeting two ladies and one man as they made their way up the front steps with dishes in hand. "You can take your food into the kitchen and then follow the arrows up the stairs to the coat room."

The obedient threesome followed directions well and then headed to the name tag table. But something didn't seem quite right.

"Marshall," I said, "who are those people? I don't recognize them."

"I don't recognize them either, Sharon. But our class is so big. Maybe they sit on the other side of the room and we just haven't noticed them before."

They looked as though they could have been one of us. They seemed to know the drill. But something still felt strange.

"Just the same, go find out who they are," I urged.

Marshall approached the trio, who were now looking a little bewildered themselves. "Excuse me. You *are* here for the Sunday school Christmas party, aren't you?"

"Yes," they answered. However, their yes sounded more like a question than an answer. Then they asked, "This is the Sunday school class for First Baptist Church, isn't it?"

"No, ma'am," Marshall answered. "This is the party for a different church. You folks are at the wrong place."

Quickly the three embarrassed Baptists reclaimed their food, once again followed the arrows to the coat room, and hightailed it out of the McMillians' house to another Sunday school covered-dish gathering a few doors down.

Won't heaven be an interesting place? One big, perpetual, brightly lit celebration. No covered dishes will be required because God will sit us down at His banqueting table which He has prepared for us. One great thing about this party will be that when the Methodists stumble into a room full of Presbyterians, no one will feel out of place. The Episcopalians will be chewing the fat with the Primitive Baptists, the Assemblies of God will be singing with the Lutherans, and the Church of God folks will be dancing with the Congregationalists.

And when each new saint arrives, we'll hear, "Welcome! Come on in. Take your coat off and stay a while—an eternity, for that matter. You're definitely in the right place."

Dear Lord, forgive us for how we have separated ourselves as believers. Help us to see each brother and sister in Christ as dearly loved children of God. In Jesus' name, amen.

ADDITIONAL SCRIPTURE READING:
GALATIANS 3:1-12; 3:26–4:7

27

No Neighbors!

Encourage one another and build each other up,
just as in fact you are doing.

1 THESSALONIANS 5:11

She was furious! She was mad! And she let me know it!
Many years ago, a neighbor was angry with me for correcting her child. She called and told me what a terrible person I was. Who did I think I was correcting her little angel? I will not go into detail about the phone call, but let's just say it was less than flattering. I did apologize but came up with a new game plan for dealing with neighbors.

"Lord, here's the deal. I am not going to get to know any of my neighbors. I am going to keep to myself, stay in my own yard, and play with my own toys. I'm going to remove the welcome mat at the front door and make sure the alarm system warning sticker is displayed in a prominent place. No borrowing a cup of sugar. No talking over the fence. No anything. I am even going to import Steven's playmates. This 'Say No to Neighbors' policy is in effect immediately."

The next day, my son went to a YMCA basketball camp on the other side of town. At pickup time, we moms were standing around talking while waiting for our sons. A beautiful blonde was standing near me, and I heard someone ask her where she lived.

"I have just moved from the Myers Park area of town to Stratfordshire Drive in the Matthews area." Then she looked over at me and smiled.

That was my street! She knew I had heard her, and she knew I lived on that street! We had not met yet because they had moved in while we were on vacation. I politely returned the smile and felt panic creeping in. What was I to do? My new policy had been in effect for less than 48 hours.

I told God I would introduce myself but reminded Him of my "Say No to Neighbors" policy. After all, I did not want to be rude, just distant (or safe). I introduced myself to Debi, welcomed her to the neighborhood, and chatted for a few minutes. Then I grabbed my son by the shirt and scurried away.

That afternoon there was a knock at the door. When I looked out of the window, who should be standing on my porch? None other than my new cheerful neighbor, Debi, "just dropping by to say hello." As I opened the door, I again reminded the Lord of my plan, just in case He had forgotten. My guard stayed up for about five minutes after she strolled through the door.

She walked in the sunroom and exclaimed, "Oh, look, we have the same china pattern. And I see you like to collect bunnies. I just love bunnies, don't you? I have them all over my house. Oh, look, we even have some of the same bunnies!"

We discovered we both enjoyed decorative flags, and we both had one for each month of the year. Then with a luminous smile Debi said, "You know, when we moved in and I saw the cute flag with firecrackers hanging by your porch, I just knew we would be friends."

And we have been ever since that day. We go to flea markets together and reach for the same items. We paint together, look for bargains together, and go on garden tours together. When her Welsh corgi, Ginny, had puppies, she named its firstborn after me. And suddenly, although I had been very capable before, I could not make any home decorating decision without first getting Debi's opinion.

My "Say No to Neighbors" plan lasted less than two days. Since then I have opened my heart and home to other neighbors, and many have become my extended family. Aren't you glad God ignores our silly resolves to keep the doors to our hearts shut tight? I just love how He continues to bring women together for mutual support and encouragement. As a matter of fact, I think friendship was one of God's best ideas.

Listen closely. Is God nudging you to reach out to a neighbor today? You might be surprised what a blessing opening your home can be.

⌐

Dear God, thank You for my friends. Thank You for
ignoring my silly antics to protect my heart against the

*possible pain of relationships. You never intended for Your
children to live in isolation, but in community. Show me
someone I can reach out to today. In Jesus' name, amen.*

ADDITIONAL SCRIPTURE READING: 1 THESSALONIANS 4:13–5:11

28

Confidence to Bank On

I can do everything through Him who gives me strength.
PHILIPPIANS 4:19

"Now, girls," the instructor said, "don't act nervous when the patients come into the clinic. If you act nervous, you'll make the patients nervous. Act confident, even if you're not."

I cringed at the instructor's words as I prepared to see my first patient in dental hygiene school. Being a very insecure person, I saw that it was imperative that I learn how to act confident, even when I wasn't.

For the first semester I didn't have to worry about appearing confident because we just worked on a mannequin, whose name was Dexter. But then came real patients. I found that real people were different from my friend Dexter. They did not have levers on the tops of their heads to pull when I wanted them to open, and I could not fold up their tongue or pin it to their cheeks when it got in the way. And it was up to me to make these real people feel comfortable.

I made it through dental hygiene school, and the art of acting confident, even when I wasn't, proved very useful on several occasions in my adult life.

My husband, Steve, and I got married while we were still in college and had little funds for a honeymoon. With yard sale money, we took a quick trip to the Outer Banks of North Carolina, just a few hours from my hometown. On our seventh anniversary, we decided to finally take that honeymoon trip, a cruise in the Bahamas. It was my job to make most of the travel preparations, which included purchasing traveler's checks from the bank. I had never used traveler's checks and didn't really know what to do. I didn't even know what a traveler's check looked like.

At this point my "Act confident even if you don't know what you are doing" training kicked in. I walked in the bank and confidently, as though I had done this a million times, announced to the teller, "Excuse me, I would like to buy some traveler's checks."

Without looking up she asked, "What denomination?"

I thought that was a strange question, but answered, "Presbyterian. We go to a Presbyterian church."

The teller looked up, the corners of her lips curled into a sardonic grin as she said, "No, honey. I mean, do you want your checks in twenties or fifties?"

My confidence level plummeted. I felt myself shrinking before the teller's very eyes as she enlightened me on a new word for the day. As I tried to find my voice, I squeaked, "Twenties will be fine." As she prepared the traveler's checks, I tried to remember the Bible verses about money changers. I did not like this woman.

I got my traveler's checks, in denominations of twenty, and crawled out of the bank, never to return. I was sure she was telling everyone what I said. She probably still tells that story at office parties and family reunions.

As I sat in my car, I began to pray. "Lord, I didn't do too well today," I whispered. Then I heard His still, small voice speak to my heart, *Sharon, you will never have true confidence until you understand who you are in Me.*

Thus began my journey of discovering who I was, what I had, and where I was as a child of God. It was a pivotal moment in my life, and I can promise you, if you haven't grasped your true identity in Christ, it will be a pivotal point in your life as well.

You are a chosen, holy, precious, dearly loved child of God who is equipped by Your heavenly Father, empowered by the Holy Spirit, and enveloped in Jesus Christ. That's real confidence, and you can take it to the bank!

⌐

Dear God, You are my confidence. I know I can do very
little on my own strength, but because of the power of the
Holy Spirit that You have placed in me, I can do everything
You have called me to do. In Jesus' name, amen.

ADDITIONAL SCRIPTURE READING: PHILIPPIANS 4:4-20

29

A Watched Pot Never Burns

She watches over the affairs of her household.

PROVERBS 31:27

Another tea kettle, burnt to a crisp!

You've heard the expression, "A watched pot never boils." Well, I must say I've taken that to heart, and as a result I've burned many pots of water. How do you burn water, you ask? It's simple. First you put water in a pot, place the pot on the stove, and turn the dial to "high." Because the water will not boil if you watch it, you leave the room to answer the telephone, fold a load of laundry, or run out to get the mail. One thing leads to another, and 30 minutes later you remember the boiling water. When you return, you discover an angry, empty pot, burnt to a blackened crisp. This result is most wonderfully observed when overheating a copper bottom pot for at least one hour. Once you burn a pot, no matter how hard you scrub, everything you cook in it afterwards comes out a little on the gray side.

Each time I have ruined a pot and had to throw it away, I've vowed to watch over the next one more carefully. But, inevitably, the phone rings or someone comes to the door, and voilà—another pot fatality.

After six of these catastrophes, the discarded pots were eating into my household budget. So I decided to buy a tea kettle that whistled. I thought, *What a pleasant little song my kettle will sing as she notifies me it's time for tea.* It was so cute with its shiny new curved handle and round copper bottom. However, the song it sang was anything but sweet. When the steam built up, the kettle let out an angry shrill that made my dog howl and my family yell at me to "get that thing off of there!" When my little teakettle got all steamed up and I heard her shout, I had to sprint from wherever I was in the house to avoid my family's complaints. There were no more burnt pots—but the new kettle was not pleasant.

After a few months of ear-piercing reminders and mad dashes to the kitchen, I made a new discovery. I found that if I pushed the button that made the teakettle's spout open just halfway down and a smidgen to the right, it would catch on the lip of the spout and stay open just far enough to let the steam out so it wouldn't whistle.

You can guess what happened. After two weeks of outsmarting the whistler, I left the room and returned to an angry charred pot rocking back and forth on the stove's hot eye. After she cooled off, she went to pot heaven along with the others.

Of course, we all know that a watched pot will indeed boil—sooner or later. But it's our patience that seems to have trouble. Watching seems like such a terrible waste of time, but that's not what Scripture says. Shepherds "watched" over their flocks by night. Guardsmen "watched" over their people by patrolling the city walls. And the Proverbs 31 woman "watched" over the affairs of her household.

The woman who is in the business of "watching over the affairs of her household" is one who is guarding, protecting, saving, and attending to the people most precious to her. And that certainly is no waste of time. We watch over the physical needs of our family. But more importantly, we watch over their emotional and spiritual needs. We bathe them in prayer, listen to their successes and failures, and pay attention to their outside interests and friends. We may never know how many disasters have been averted by a mother's prayers, availability, and nurturing care.

What is God urging you to watch and wait for today? It could be one of the hardest and most rewarding tasks you'll ever do.

⌒

Dear God, today I lift up my family. I pray for their protection,
their provision, and their path. As I go through my busy
day, please prompt me to pay attention to their needs and
be in tune with their hearts' desires. In Jesus' name, amen.

ADDITIONAL SCRIPTURE READING: PROVERBS 31:10-31

30

Forgiving Karl

Forgive as the Lord forgave you.

COLOSSIANS 3:13

Trish Campbell's life was bursting with promise. Her son, Wayne, was home from Camden South Carolina Military Academy. The 16-year-old cadet had just received his driver's license and a shiny new truck. In just four days, Trish would be marrying Teddy and then honeymooning on an Alaskan cruise. Life was good.

Wayne had plans to spend the weekend with one of his best friends from the Academy, Karl. Karl had recently graduated from Camden and was scheduled to start classes at The Citadel in the fall. He was an "A" student and graduated second in his class at Camden. He was president of the honor society and the fine arts club, lieutenant governor of the Key Club for North and South Carolina, captain of the soccer and wrestling teams, and company commander to 65 cadets in his senior year.

Trish liked Karl. He was outgoing, polite, and seemed responsible. She also trusted his parents. His father was a pastor at a large church, and his mother was a former school board member.

Trish didn't feel comfortable with Wayne driving his new truck out of town in rush hour traffic to Karl's, so she rode along with him as her fiancé followed behind to bring her back home.

"I love you," she said repeatedly before leaving Wayne at Karl's home.

"I love you too, Mom," he replied as he hugged her several times.

What Trish didn't know was that the boys had a secret. Nineteen-year-old Karl and his friends had planned a party. They had the place—a nearby field. They had an alibi—a lie that they were spending the night with a friend. They had a keg of beer—purchased by an older boy.

Around midnight Karl and his best friend, Wayne, jumped into a Jeep. Karl was at the wheel. About a quarter of a mile from the party,

Karl's Jeep drifted left. He overcorrected and cut a hard right, then back to the left. The Jeep and the driver were out of control. The right-side tires blew and the rims dug into the road. Then the Jeep flipped and ejected Wayne about 50 feet onto the pavement. Karl's upper lip was torn and hanging, but he still did not understand the gravity of the situation. For the first time he realized he might be drunk.

The tranquility of the early Sunday morning was pierced by sirens, the swooshing of a rescue helicopter, and wailing of young adults. As the helicopter airlifted Wayne to the hospital, Karl rode in the ambulance. But Wayne never left the hospital. Six days after he had arrived, Wayne Campbell, the only son of Trish Campbell, died.

Several months later, Karl had his day in court, facing a charge of involuntary manslaughter and possible prison time. One by one, men and women stood and testified on Karl's behalf—his soccer coach, his teachers, and his Sunday school teacher. After the prosecutor presented his case, Trish asked if she could address the court. Permission was granted.

"My son and Karl went to school together and were best friends," Trish began. "I love this boy like my own child. It's *not* my wish that he should serve prison time. I understand that he will have some type of punishment, and I accept that. But I know Karl is truly remorseful and never intended for this to happen.

"I am a sinner, and God sent His only Son to save me and forgive me of my sins. I'm not worthy of that forgiveness. So why wouldn't I forgive Karl?"

Those who stood by to hear and see the interaction were startled at such forgiveness and grace pouring from this woman. It was not human. It was divine.

I know this family. I lived this story. My heart breaks even now thinking of precious Karl and the pain he has had to suffer for one bad choice. But you know what? We all make bad choices every day. His came at a very high price.

I see myself in Karl. No, I haven't been convicted of involuntary manslaughter while driving impaired, but I've done other things that have been detrimental to people's souls...and to my own. And then I see Wayne's mother approach the bench on Karl's behalf, and I see Jesus approach the bench on my behalf.

"Judge," He would say. "I love this woman like she is my own...she *is* my own. I know she will have consequences here on earth for the poor choices she has made. But I do not want her to serve any jail time. I ask that You extend mercy and grace to this woman, that You commute her sentence and set her free."

Then the gavel comes down and the Judge announces to the court, "No jail time. She's free."

How about you? Have you accepted God's grace and forgiveness in your life? Is there someone you need to forgive today?

Dear God, thank You for forgiving me and wiping my slate clean. Help me to show that same mercy and grace to others as I forgive quickly and completely. In Jesus' name, amen.

ADDITIONAL SCRIPTURE READING: COLOSSIANS 3:1-17

31

Chosen

In him we were also chosen.

EPHESIANS 1:11

K.C. was a beautiful blonde freshman at Georgia State University. She was excited to be at college and looked forward to having a fresh start at life. When rush week came around, she was the first to sign up. This was the week when all the girls desiring to become a member of a sorority went from Greek house to Greek house, mingling and hoping to be chosen to become a "sister." After the tiring week of parties, constant smiling, and small talk, the girls waited anxiously until the Friday night party to find out who chose them. K.C. began getting dressed for the celebration when the phone rang.

"Hello," she answered cheerfully.

"Hi, K.C., this is Cassie, the rush coordinator. I'm sorry to tell you this, but looking at the list, no one chose you."

Those words, "No one chose you," rang in K.C.'s ears for years.

K.C. isn't the only one who has felt the sting of rejection. We all have. Even King David in the Bible, the "man after God's own heart," felt the pain of being shunned by his own family.

After God took the kingship away from Saul, He sent the prophet Samuel to anoint the next king of Israel. By God's instruction, Samuel traveled to Bethlehem to the house of Jesse. Samuel knew where to go and what family the king would come from. He knew the next king would be one of Jesse's sons…he just didn't know *which* son.

Samuel arrived in Bethlehem and asked Jesse to bring all of his sons out for his inspection. Jesse brought out each of his seven sons, one by one. As Samuel prayerfully approached each young man, God said, "No, that is not the one… No, that is not the one… No, that is not the one…" Seven times God refused Jesse's sons. Finally, exasperated and confused, Samuel asked Jesse, "Are these all the sons you have?"

"Oh, yeah. I do have one more son," Jesse said. "I almost forgot all about him. Little David is out taking care of the sheep. I'll send someone to get him."

David was so insignificant to his own father that when the prophet requested an audience with *all* of his boys, Jesse didn't even think to invite him. However, David was the very one God had selected to be the next ruler of His chosen people. How exciting! You may have felt overlooked, disregarded, and ignored, but God has chosen you to be His child.

After a conference where I was speaking about our new identity in Christ, K.C. told me this story about being rejected by the sororities at her school. She had never told anyone before, but now she was free from the pain of those words.

"For the first time in my life I can let go of that pain because I realize I *was* chosen. God chose me. He chose *me*. So what if those girls didn't. God chose me, and that's much more impressive than a sorority pin."

God chose *you*, precious friend. Like a groom who chooses, pursues, and captures the love of his life, He chose you!

⌐

Heavenly Father, thank You for choosing me! No matter how many times I may feel rejection in this life, I will rejoice that You chose me to be Your precious child. In Jesus' name, amen.

ADDITIONAL SCRIPTURE READING: EPHESIANS 1:1-23

32

Trick Skis

When they measure themselves by themselves
and compare themselves with themselves, they are not wise.

2 CORINTHIANS 10:12

"Slow down!" I yelled as Steve barreled down the snow-covered mountain.

I am not, and never have been, a very athletic person. I think I have "ball-phobia." If it's round and moves, I can't hit it, or catch it, or kick it. My husband, on the other hand, can catch, throw, shoot, or drive a ball of any shape and size to hit its mark.

The one thing I can do athletically is snow ski. For some reason, that just came naturally to me, probably because there is no ball involved. When Steve and I started dating, I offered to teach him how. He was aware of my athletic capabilities, or lack thereof, and decided that if I could do it, he could do it.

We went to Sugar Mountain, North Carolina, for his first lesson. The key moves to learn when you first hit the slopes are how to slow down, how to stop, and how to get up once you fall. The first thing Steve learned was how to get up, because the first thing he did was fall.

To slow down, I taught Steve to turn his skis sideways and crisscross back and forth across the mountain, instead of going straight down. He would go straight for a while, and then when his speed picked up, Steve would turn his skis sideways to slow down. The only problem was, he had a tendency to turn too far to the side and ended up with the skis pointing up the mountain. Inevitably, he would then begin sliding downhill backward. This was not good!

Finally, he came up with a plan. "When I try to turn, if I turn too much, I can just continue turning 360 degrees, making a complete circle. That will still slow me down and I won't end up going downhill backward." So that's what he did. It was a sight to behold, but it worked.

Toward the end of the day a woman approached Steve and asked,

"Sir, I have been watching your beautiful acrobatics all day long. Can you teach me how to make those wonderful circles in the snow?"

Steve laughed and obliged.

She thought he was an expert skier and didn't realize he was just going in circles to survive.

Isn't that the way life is sometimes? We look at other people and think they have it all together. *Oh, if I could just handle life the way she does,* we muse. *If I just had an orderly home like her, well-mannered children like her, a loving husband like her.* In reality, she is most likely going in circles, just like you are, doing whatever it takes not to go downhill backwards.

But as children of God, we don't have to go in circles. We simply need to rely on His power, rest in His strength, and keep our heart attuned to His leading. And, perhaps, when someone asks, "Can you show me how to depend on God like you do?" we'll be able to oblige.

Do you sometimes feel as though you are going in circles? I know I do. Let's agree with David, who wrote: "Teach me to do your will, for you are my God; may your good Spirit lead me on level ground" (Psalm 143:10).

⌒

Dear God, forgive me for comparing myself to others. I know You made me unique in every way. Help me to be the best me I can be and live my life for an audience of One...You! In Jesus' name, amen.

ADDITIONAL SCRIPTURE READING: 2 CORINTHIANS 10:12-18

33

Swollen Imaginations

*Finally, brothers and sisters,
whatever is true...think about such things.*

PHILIPPIANS 4:8 TNIV

It was a miracle! She was healed! At least her imagination was, anyway.
Ada had an uneventful dental visit at my husband's office—just
a routine filling. He was surprised when she called him at home later
that evening, complaining of a swollen cheek and excruciating pain.

"Dr. Jaynes," she groaned. "I can barely hold my head up. My face
is swollen, I can't open my mouth, and the pain is severe."

"Ada, I'm so sorry you're having trouble," Steve replied. "I can't
imagine what the problem could be. I'll call in some pain medicine for
you, and please come to the office first thing in the morning."

The following day I was working as Steve's assistant, and I was
amazed at Ada's appearance when she arrived at the office. Her eyes
were half closed, she could barely walk, and her right cheek did appear
quite swollen. Ada sat down in the chair as if every movement took
great effort. She could barely open her mouth to let Steve see what the
problem might be. Finally she did manage to open slightly. Steve gently lifted her lip and a huge grin spread across his face. He reached in
with an instrument and removed a cotton roll from the area between
her cheek and tooth.

Ada's eyes popped open as she miraculously bolted upright in the
chair. "What did you do?" she exclaimed, all signs of weakness gone.
Ada was miraculously healed!

Steve grinned and held up the small piece of cotton. "This is what
was causing you so much 'pain.'"

Ada was terribly embarrassed.

Steve and I replayed the scenes from the previous day. Before placing the filling, he put a small cotton roll between Ada's cheek and tooth
to keep the area dry. I was assisting him that day and forgot to remove

the cotton roll when he had finished. When the anesthesia wore off, Ada felt her cheek and thought it was swollen. As the night wore on, her imagination ran rampant until she had worked herself into such a state that she could barely move from the imaginary pain. She had made herself sick. Never once did she open her mouth and look inside. If she had, she would have seen a little white piece of cotton.

That is the power of imagination. We can literally worry ourselves sick over something that isn't even real. The apostle Paul said we need to take every thought captive to make it obedient to Christ (2 Corinthians 10:5). Just like the policeman who pursues and captures a criminal on the loose, we can capture those runaway thoughts and lock them away for good.

Do you have any runaway thoughts, fears, or worries that need to be captured and removed from your mind today? If you're not sure, open up to God and let Him take a look.

Dear God, sometimes I blow situations way out of proportion. Keep me from allowing my imagination to run rampant with worries and fears, and help me to remember that You have everything under control. In Jesus' name, amen.

ADDITIONAL SCRIPTURE READING: PHILIPPIANS 4:4-9

34

Barking! Barking! Barking!

Let us fix our eyes on Jesus,
the author and perfecter of our faith.

HEBREWS 12:2

There it goes again—the tidal wave of barking. Even when I'm tucked away on my patio behind my house, I can tell when a neighbor is going for a walk or a jogger is jaunting down the street. It starts with Mitzi, the white cockapoo one block away. Yip. Yip. Yip. Then it moves two houses down with Duchess, the black Labrador. Bow. Wow. Wow. The wave continues to move closer with Pal, the standard poodle. Arf. Arf. Arf. And onto Sprout, the collie. Woof. Woof. Woof.

Then the pedestrian turns off Stratfordshire Drive onto my side street, Trafalgar. All of a sudden, the doggie hallelujah chorus breaks out with my dog, Ginger; Alice, the white lab; Maple, the Heinz 57 across the street; and another Duchess, the German shepherd next door. I usually don't see the passerby, but I can surely hear the snarls and insults from the dogs as he or she strolls along.

When I take my routine three-mile walk through the neighborhood, I too am greeted by the wave of barking dogs indignant that I should dare pass by their turf. I try not to let it hurt my feelings. However, the chain reaction of barking, jeering, growling, and gnashing of teeth never ceases to unnerve me.

The truth is, I wish the pups would wag their tails as I walk by, as if to say, "Oh, there's that sweet Mrs. Jaynes. My, how I like her. I wish she were my master and we could take walks together. Mrs. Jaynes! Mrs. Jaynes! Won't you please come over and pat my head?" I wish they would run up to the fence, jump up sweetly, and let their waving tails beckon me to stop for a visit. But for the 20 years I have walked the same route, this has never happened. It's always growl, ruff, and bark. You'd think I would have gotten use to it, but I never did.

I hate to admit it, but it's been the same way in life from time to time. As I've walked down the path of years, especially down that road less traveled, I have heard some unfriendly barking, some disapproving jeering, and a few disdainful growls. Sometimes it's a complaint because I'm not living up to someone's expectations. Sometimes it's because I'm not following someone else's plan for my life. And sometimes it's because I'm coloring outside people-imposed lines.

But let's just stop and call it what it is. Barking. Yapping. Howling.

Thankfully, there are other sounds I notice during my walks in the neighborhood: the laughing of children, the ringing of church bells, the humming of lawnmowers, the singing of birds, the encouragement of a friend, the melody of a piano, the whispers of God. On which will I choose to focus? Opponents will bark, but God will send cheers.

He is saying, *Oh, how I love you, My precious child. I love walking with you in the cool of the morning and in the dusk of the evening. I see your efforts to follow My path, and I have provided a great cloud of witnesses to cheer you on. Your name is written in the palm of My hand—not so I won't forget it, but because I have held you so tightly that you have left a lasting impression there. Keep walking. You are doing well.*

There will always be those who bark, but let's listen for the sounds of heaven that cheer us on.

Lord, help me to listen to Your still, small voice today. Thank You for loving me, guiding me, and cheering me on as I walk through this life by Your side. In Jesus' name, amen.

ADDITIONAL SCRIPTURE READING: HEBREWS 11:1-40–12:1-3

35

Bushwhacked

Every branch that does bear fruit he prunes
so that it will be even more fruitful.

JOHN 15:2

"Honey," my husband announced. "It's time to cut back the bushes." After ten years, our lush bushes were at their peak of fullness and beauty. And now my husband planned on cutting them back! To bare branches! No way!

"No, please don't," I cried. "They look so pretty right now."

"Sharon, they look great on the outside," he explained, "but inside they are bare. Cutting them back so the sun can reach the inside will make them healthier and fuller in the long run."

Reluctantly, I submitted to Rambo and his hedge trimmer as he bushwhacked my beautiful shrubs. The bushes looked like shaved dogs standing sentinel around our house. They almost seemed embarrassed, standing there naked and bare. Ugly. That's what they were. Ugly.

However, in about two months, little green leaves began emerging from the remaining branches, and within a few more weeks the bushes were healthier and more beautiful than before.

Through that process God began to show me that sometimes I need a good trimming. Sometimes I can get so involved in ministry and life that my insides grow a bit bare. I might look spiritually healthy on the outside, but on the inside, where it really counts, I may be languishing…sometimes without even knowing it. So God comes along with His holy hedge trimmers and begins lopping off the beautiful branches.

"What are You doing?" I might cry.

Don't worry, He replies. *You'll feel bare for a time, but in the end you'll be even healthier and more spiritually beautiful than before.*

I've grown accustomed to Steve and his dogged determination to cut the bushes back. And I've grown accustomed to God's perfect pruning in my life as well.

How about you? Are there some areas of your life that need a good holy bushwhacking? Ask God to show you if there are some activities and commitments that should go in order to make room for new growth in your life.

Dear God, I don't like pruning. But today I am asking You to prune away everything in my life that is hindering me from blooming into the spiritually beautiful woman You created me to be. In Jesus' name, amen.

ADDITIONAL SCRIPTURE READING: JOHN 15:1-17

36

A Masterpiece Restored

Create in me a clean heart, O God,
and renew a steadfast spirit within me.

PSALM 51:10 NASB

W e want our paintings back!" they cried. "We want them to stay the way they've always been!"

In 2002 my family traveled to Europe and visited one of the greatest artistic masterpieces in the history of man—the Sistine Chapel. Many artists contributed to the paintings, tapestries, and sculptures within its walls, but the most magnificent feat is the ceiling painted by Michelangelo. From 1508 to 1512, Michelangelo lay on his back and painstakingly painted one gigantic spiritual, historical, and biblical account of man. But almost as soon as the paintings were completed, they began to fade. After years of fading, ill attempts to cover the paintings with varnish, and layers of smoke and dirt, the original masterpiece was barely visible.

But in 1981 a special cleaning solution called AB-57 was discovered. The Italian proprietors of this historical and spiritual international treasure decided to test a new process for cleaning the murals that lined the walls and ceilings. They were surprised by the vibrant colors that emerged when years of filth and grime were gingerly removed. The process of cleaning the ceiling, inch by inch, took eight years, twice as long as it had taken Michelangelo to paint. Artisans were amazed and awed at the beauty, the colors, and the intricate details as the paintings were brought back to life. For the first time in nearly 500 years, spectators saw the masterpiece the way it was originally intended.

But not everyone was pleased with the restoration. Some of the locals rebelled at the newly restored works of art. They had become accustomed to the dulling filth and grime left by years of pollution and cried, "We want our paintings back!"

It was difficult for me to fathom anyone not appreciating the vivid colors the original artists intended. Then God reminded me of His desire for our total restoration, and of how some of His children are much more comfortable with the years of filth and grime that mar His original works of art. Yes, God has dreams for our lives, but many times years of disappointment and pain pollute and mask those dreams. God's desire is to wash us clean and restore the dreams He had when He created His original work of art in the Garden of Eden. Can we bear the beauty? Are we ready for the vibrant colors of a fulfilling and exciting life in Christ?

God is the great Restorer, and He is in the process of creating a breathtaking masterpiece—you, an original work of art. Are you ready for a change? I know I am.

Heavenly Father, I don't want to stay the way I've always been. Clean me up! Make me new! Restore me to the way You originally intended me to be before sin and shame entered into the world. Create in me a clean heart, O God, and restore a right spirit within me. In Jesus' name, amen.

ADDITIONAL SCRIPTURE READING: PSALM 51:1-19

37

Who's the Boss?

This is love for God: to obey his commands.

1 JOHN 5:3

No," he said when I told him to put on his coat. "No," he responded when I told him to take a bath. "No," he said when I told him to wash his hands.

For two months Alex, a ten-year-old foreign exchange student from Russia, became part of our family. As soon as he walked off of the airplane and into our lives, it became apparent that this was more than a foreign exchange experience for him. He was on vacation from authority—from all authority.

I suspect Alex's comprehension of the English language was a lot better than he let on. Even though his command of the language was tentative, his command of the word "no" was secure. When I made a request, such as "Alex, put on your jacket," he would look me in the eye and say, "No." Whether it was "Alex, comb your hair," or "Alex, eat your breakfast," I was always met with a stern-faced "No." However, my job was to teach him that in America, parents are boss—at least, that's the way it should be. So I just kept repeating my requests until one of us grew tired. It was never me.

My requests were not unreasonable, but one particular request met with great opposition each time. It was "Alex, now it's time to take a bath." Once, however, Alex complied with the bath time request without one single argument. *Now we're getting somewhere,* I thought. After he ran the bathwater, I walked by the bathroom to check on him, only to find him standing by the bathtub, fully clothed, waiting for the proper amount of time to pass before letting the water out. What a lot of trouble to go through just to avoid a bath!

My son, Steven, had always been a fairly compliant child. However, at age two, his favorite word was also "no." But by age three, he had learned that "in America parents are boss." So this strong will in Alex was new to me, but I was up for the challenge and did not waver.

The two months passed. Alex got back on the plane with new clothes, new shoes, and other new American merchandise. I'm not sure how much he learned about the American Christian family, but I learned a lot about the word "no."

When a two-year-old looks you in the eye and puckers up his sweet little cherry lips to form the word "no," even though it has to be dealt with, you have to admit that it's kind of cute. However, when a ten-year-old looks you in the eye and unabashedly forms that same word, it's not cute any longer. How must the Lord feel when we adults plant our feet, with hands on our hips, and say no to Him? How foolish are we to refuse our loving Parent's commands? But, because He loves us, He'll keep repeating the commands until we figure out that He's the Boss who always has our best interests in mind.

What's He saying to you today? What is your response?

⌐

Heavenly Father, please forgive me when I have ignored Your commands. Please forgive me for the times I've said no to You. Help me to be an obedient child who obeys quickly and completely. In Jesus' name, amen.

ADDITIONAL SCRIPTURE READING: 1 JOHN 5:1-12

38

Mining for Gold

When he has tested me, I will come forth as gold.

JOB 23:10

If there is one thing I know about mining for gold, it's this: You often have to push through a lot of dirt to find it.

I knelt beside a creek bed, surrounded by 30 fourth graders panning for gold. We were at Reid Gold Mine, and I was the chaperone of the rowdy young miners. The tour guide took us through dark musty tunnels, explaining how the miners a hundred years ago had searched for veins of gold imbedded in the rocks and hidden beneath the sodden walls. Many tirelessly panned for gold in the chilled mountain stream in hopes of finding a few valuable nuggets. Some struck it rich; others left empty-handed.

After the tour we each grabbed a sieve and tried our luck at panning for gold. First we lowered our pans into the mud of the streambed and filled our sieves. Then we shook the pans back and forth, allowing the crystal clear water to flow over their contents. The silt and dirt filtered through the screen and fell back into the stream as hopeful children (and a few adults) searched for gold.

As I knelt beside the flowing water and filled my pan with mud, God began to speak to my heart. He began to show me that my life had been very similar to panning for gold. Yes, there was dirt. Yes, there was mud. But as I allowed God's Spirit to wash over the painful memories, I discovered valuable nuggets of gold in the form of life lessons.

Even though I didn't discover a treasure in my sieve that day, nuggets of gold began to fill my mind. Diamonds in darkness. Pearls in pain. Rubies in rough times.

Our lives, no matter how messy, are filled with valuable nuggets of gold. We simply need to look beyond the dirt and allow God to expose the treasures just waiting to be discovered. And then when we do, we will have a storehouse of truths to share with those around us. Who knows? Maybe God will use you to be a gold miner in someone else's life, or at least lead them to the stream to find treasures of their own.

Dear God, my life has been littered with messes. Thank You for helping me sift through the dirt to discover nuggets of gold hiding below the surface. Help me be a miner who always pans for gold in the muddiness of life and then turns to invest her discoveries in the lives of others. In Jesus' name, amen.

ADDITIONAL SCRIPTURE READING: ROMANS 5:1-5; JAMES 1:2-4

39

A Dainty Morsel

The perverse stir up dissension,
and gossips separate close friends.

PROVERBS 16:28 TNIV

A monster was coming into my yard in the dark of night and eating my plants. I never saw him—just the aftermath of his destruction. He left a trail of slime as he moved from plant to plant, leaving gaping holes in broad-leaved gerbera daisies, gnawing entire velvety trumpet-shaped blossoms on purple petunias, and reducing bushy begonias to naked stalks.

Morning after morning I awoke to discover that the monster had consumed yet another beautiful flower. Something had to be done. I wasn't sure if I needed a bear trap, a stun gun, or a torpedo, but I was determined to capture this gargantuan beast.

I asked a neighbor about my garden's demise. She took one look at the ravaged foliage and the slimy trail glistening in the sunlight. "You have slugs," she said.

"Slugs!" I exclaimed. "The yard monster is a tiny little slug?"

"You can put out slug bait to catch them and see for yourself," she confidently continued.

I sprinkled slug bait all around the yard and then waited. The next morning I viewed the monsters' remains. The beasts were a quarter inch long—about the size of my little toenail.

How could something so small cause so much damage in such a short amount of time? I mused. Then God reminded me of something else very small that can cause enormous damage in a short amount of time… gossip. King Solomon wrote: "The words of a gossip are like choice morsels; they go down to a man's inmost part" (Proverbs 18:8). Just as one tiny slug can destroy a flower bed, so one tiny morsel of gossip can destroy a person's reputation, mar someone's character, and devour a friendship.

It takes two to tango, and it takes two to gossip: one to repeat a matter and one to listen. That's one dance we don't need to enter into at all. Let's sit that one out and listen to what God has to say instead.

~

Dear Lord, help me not to gossip today. And if I feel the urge to do so, I pray You will put Your holy hand over my mouth and keep the words from passing my lips. In Jesus' name, amen.

ADDITIONAL SCRIPTURE READING: PROVERBS 16:21-28

40

Faulty Wiring

The driving is like the driving of Jehu the son
of Nimshi, for he drives furiously.

2 KINGS 9:20 NASB

I hope that verse made you smile. I'll bet you know a few folks who drive furiously. Well, for several years, people looked at me and thought I drove anything but furiously.

In a 15-year period I owned four different cars—each and every one a blue station wagon. They weren't the same make, mind you, but blue station wagons nonetheless. Three of the four blue "mommy cars" had some serious issues. One had her wires crossed and the electrical system was all confused, one overheated constantly and left me stranded on the side of the road often, and one had a sluggish speedometer.

Of the four wagons, the Quantum was the most attractive. She was dark blue, had a slim figure, and moved with an air of sophistication. If I was going to drive a "mommy wagon," I decided to do it with a bit of class.

Shortly after I bought this car, I noticed that drivers in Charlotte were getting more aggressive every day. Indignant commuters flew up behind me and rode on my bumper, impatient teenagers passed me on the straightaways at amazing speed, and highway travelers flew around me as though they had their pilot's license.

"What's wrong with these people?" I complained. "These drivers are so irresponsible!"

"Look at that woman on my bumper!" I exclaimed.

"What's your problem?" I fretted.

"Man, that teenager is so reckless. I have a good mind to write down his license plate number and call his mom," I mumbled.

"Good grief. That car's going at least 85 and the speed limit is 60. What does he think this is? A race track? I hope he gets a ticket. He sure deserves one," I said.

I decided I was not going to succumb to the recklessness of other drivers but maintain a safe speed and follow the rules. All the while, I puttered along, proud of myself for obeying the law.

One day Steve and I went to visit some friends in a nearby city. We met Mike at the church where he worked and then proceeded to follow him on the highway back to his house. After traveling about ten miles or so, Mike slowed down to drive beside us, rolled down his window, and yelled, "What's wrong with your car?"

"Nothing. Why?" Steve yelled back through his open window.

"Because you're going 45 miles per hour when the speed limit is 55."

"No, we're not. We're going 55."

"No, buddy. You're going 45."

Then I had an "aha" moment. Is this why cars have been passing us as though we were a mule in a horse race? Is this why our last trip to the coast took five hours instead of the usual four?

"Mike," Steve yelled, "you get in front of us and go 55. We'll keep up with you."

Mike pulled out in front and held steady at 55 mph. We followed close behind. Our speedometer read 65 mph.

Steve pulled up beside Mike and yelled out the window. "Now go 65."

Again, we followed our friend. Our speedometer read 80 mph!

When we returned to Charlotte, we took the car into the dealership for an examination. The mechanic discovered that the speedometer was improperly set. When we were going 30 mph, it read 35. When we were going 45 mph, it read 55. When we were going 65, it read 80. The faster the car went, the more the mph indicator was off.

All those months I had been complaining about bad drivers. I judged people by my measuring stick, but my measuring stick was way off. I made faulty judgments based on a wrong perception of the truth. All the while I was the one with the problem.

How many times do we make up our own list of rules and regulations when God simply says, "Follow Me?" How many times do we urge fellow travelers to "go" when God is maybe telling them to "yield"? How many times do we want to hand out a citation or turn someone in for breaking the rules, when God says, "Who are you to judge a servant of another? Pay attention to your own business."

The mechanic couldn't fix our speedometer. I had to learn how to translate what I saw on the meter to how fast I was actually going. I also learned *not* to worry about other drivers down the highways and byways of life, but to focus on my own maneuvers. After all, we're all wired differently.

∾

Dear Lord, forgive me for judging how others are driving through life. I have no idea the bumps in the road they have had to endure or the potholes in the soul they have had to maneuver around. Help me to keep my eyes on my own journey and listen to Your voice as I careen around the curves and steer down the straightaways of my busy day. In Jesus' name, amen.

ADDITIONAL SCRIPTURE READING: LUKE 11:37-52

41

Foot Holding

*My grace is sufficient for you,
for my power is made perfect in weakness.*

2 CORINTHIANS 12:9

Something strange was going on in my head, and the doctors couldn't figure out what it was. I was told, "You'll need an MRI."

I wasn't sure I wanted anyone to see what was going on inside my head, but off I went to the appointment. As the nurse prepped me and drew pictures on my head, she asked, "Are you claustrophobic?"

"No, ma'am. Not at all," I answered.

"Have you ever had a panic attack?"

"No, never."

After I was strapped into place on a metal table, the nurse left the room, pushed the magic button, and I began my journey into the metal tube. The top of the canister was four inches from my face. My entire body, except for my feet, was encased in the metal can like a hotdog in a bun. Suddenly, I couldn't breathe.

"Excuse me," I yelled. "Can you bring me out a minute?"

The nurse immediately moved the table I was lying on out of the tube and asked, "What's wrong, Mrs. Jaynes?"

"I don't know. I can't breathe!"

"You're having a panic attack. I thought you said you weren't claustrophobic—"

"I am *not* claustrophobic and I'm *not* having a panic attack," I reassured her. "Put me back in there."

Again she pushed the button and my table slid into the metal tube. Once again I couldn't breathe.

"Pull me out! I can't breathe!"

We tried covering my eyes with a towel and placing an angled mirror on the inside of the tube so I could see out. Nothing worked.

"You can't do this today," the nurse said. "You'll have to come back another day." My time and her patience were used up.

I left feeling discouraged. There had not been many things I couldn't conquer in my life, and here was something so seemingly insignificant. Lying in a metal tube for forty-five minutes while listening to a jackhammer had gotten the better of me.

I went home and told my friend Mary Ruth about my ordeal.

"I feel like such a wimp," I confessed.

"That's baloney!" she said. "You just need a friend. We'll do this together."

The next week I went back with my secret weapon (Mary Ruth). She stood at the end of the tube, held my foot, prayed, and waved like Howdy Doody. The procedure went off without a hitch.

All my life I've struggled with wanting to be self-sufficient, but through moments like these, God reminds me, "My grace is sufficient for you, for my power is made perfect in weakness." It's okay to be weak. In fact, it's more than okay. It's His plan. When we admit that we are weak, He gives us His strength.

Many times God pumps courage into us through a friend who holds our hand. In this case, He used Mary Ruth to hold my foot.

How about you? Are you trying to make things happen in your own strength or are you depending on God to be strong in your weakness today?

*God, thank You for friends. What a gift! Show me
someone who needs an encouraging word today. Help
me to be the kind of friend to others I have always
wanted for myself. In Jesus' name, amen.*

ADDITIONAL SCRIPTURE READING: 2 CORINTHIANS 12:1-10

42

Acting like a Dog

*Even though I was once a blasphemer and a
persecutor and a violent man, I was shown mercy
because I acted in ignorance and unbelief.*

1 TIMOTHY 1:13

Every room in my house, except two, has one thing in common. Somewhere, nestled beside a chair, tucked on a bookshelf, painted on a mural, crouched among bed pillows, or hiding in a houseplant, rests some type of bunny. From needlepoint to ceramic to crystal, bunnies are the mainstay in the Jaynes' decor. The only two exceptions are my son's bedroom and the recreation room. He drew a line in the carpet and dared me to put a rabbit in his personal space.

So with this love of bunnies, you can imagine how excited I was when Mrs. Cottontail decided to raise her family underneath my backyard gazebo. I didn't even mind that she helped herself to my monkey grass and snacked on my impatiens. I planted half for me to enjoy and half for Mrs. Cottontail and her offspring.

The only one who was not delighted with our guests was Ginger, our golden retriever. I tried to keep her away from the area, but once she caught a whiff of rabbit stew, there was no stopping the sniffing, pawing, and digging. Each time I caught her excavating the landscape to burrow under the gazebo, I reprimanded her sternly, "No! Ginger! Get away from there!" She obediently turned and walked away with her tail tucked between her legs. Then she hid around the corner to wait for me to walk away so she could get at it again with dirt, pine straw, and flowers flying in every direction.

We had to go away for a few days and Ginger seized the moment. I can almost picture the wheels in her head turning when she saw the wheels of our packed car pull out of the driveway. I imagine as soon as we rounded the corner of the neighborhood, she dashed to the gazebo and with dogged determination began to dig.

When we came home, we observed the fruits of her labor. Ginger had bulldozed the entire landscape around the gazebo so that it now sported its own personal moat. It was a miracle the structure was still standing at all. Flowers—gone. Mounded dirt beds—gone. Pine straw—gone. The foundation was totally exposed and the gazebo sat on cinderblocks looking like someone caught with his pants down.

While my husband was rebuilding the flower bed, one of Mrs. Cottontail's children poked its head out from under the foundation to see what all the commotion was about. Startled to be eye to eye with Steve, it hopped out from the safety of its home into the yard. Ginger was lying right by her master, and before you could say "Jack Rabbit" she had the bunny in her mouth.

"Steve!" I screamed, "Ginger has the bunny! Get it out! Get it out!"

"Ginger, no!" he yelled as he bopped her on the head. "Give me the bunny."

Reluctantly, Ginger dropped the baby bunny into Steve's gloved hand.

"I think she broke its legs," he said.

"I can't believe she did that! I don't ever want a pet that would hurt a bunny!" I said through sobs. "What kind of dog is she, anyway?"

Steve walked over and put his hand on my shoulder. "Sharon, Ginger is a dog. This is what dogs do. She's not malicious or mean-spirited. Don't be mad at her for doing what comes naturally. You can't get mad at a dog for acting like a dog."

He was right, of course. We finished repairing the landscape and put a wire fence around the gazebo to restrain Ginger's curiosity. Eventually, Ginger and I made up, and I accepted the truth that she was doing what dogs do and I shouldn't expect anything to the contrary.

It did make me think, however, of other situations where I place unrealistic expectations on people. Sometimes I expect toddlers to act like reasoning six-year-olds. Occasionally, I expect teenagers to act like adults. (I know. This is ridiculous! But I am admitting my folly.) And I have been known to expect Christians to act as though they have already received their glorified state of perfection. Why, I've even caught myself, just a time or two, expecting my husband to be omnipotent (able to meet my every whim), omnipresent (right by my side whenever I call), and omniscient (able to read my mind).

And here's a big one…I often expect someone who doesn't know Jesus to live her life as though she does.

As you go through the day, pay attention to your expectations of others. When you read the paper, watch the news, or check out the Internet, ask God to show you if you are expecting others to act like someone who has had their eyes opened by the truth of the Holy Spirit within them, when in truth they aren't even able to do so.

~

Dear Heavenly Father, forgive me for expecting those who don't know Jesus to act like those who do. When I become frustrated, prompt me to pray that their eyes will be opened to the truth of Your Word. And while You're at it, open my eyes to the truth of my behavior as well. In Jesus' name, amen.

ADDITIONAL SCRIPTURE READING: 1 CORINTHIANS 2:11-16

43

I Can't-itis

*At just the right time we will reap
a harvest of blessing if we don't give up.*

Galatians 6:9 nlt

I quit!"

Steven threw his bicycle on the ground, placed his balled up fists on his hips, and kicked the rear tire.

By the time my son was four years old, he had a bad case of "I Can't-itis." If he didn't have immediate success in an endeavor, his tendency was to throw up his chubby little hands and say, "I can't do it!"

When it came time to take the training wheels off his bike, a bad case of "I Can't-itis" crept in. He looked very doubtful as we unscrewed the extra side wheels that had balanced the bike for the past few months. In usual fashion, I held on to the back of his bike as he tried to steady himself. As soon as he saw that I had let go, down he went.

For quite a while Steven tried to balance on two wheels but crashed to the ground time and time again. "I can't do it!" he stormed.

"You can't do it *yet*," I encouraged. "But you will. And when you learn to ride your bike, it will be the *funnest* thing you do as a kid."

Steven looked me in the eye and slowly said, "This is *not* fun and it will *never* be fun."

Oh, my, how I saw myself in those eyes. So many times when God is trying to teach me a life lesson or a new discipline, I lose my balance and want to quit. He takes the training wheels off and sets me on the road of maturity, and sometimes I tumble to the ground. "I can't do it," I cry. "This is *not* fun and it will *never* be fun."

But God just keeps on working with me, holding the back of the bicycle until I learn to balance and keep moving straight ahead. The next thing you know, I'm cruising down victory lane and God is smiling with joy and delight.

A few days after Steven's declaration of defeat, he walked out the door, hopped on his little red bike, and peddled around the yard without losing his balance once. And you know what? Riding his bicycle was the *funnest* thing he ever did as a kid.

Have you ever felt a bit wobbly when embarking on a new endeavor? Have you ever quit because the task seemed too hard? Well, perhaps God is calling you to get back up and try again. Take the training wheels off. Get moving. Riding down the road to obedience will be the *funnest* thing we ever do as God's kid.

*Dear God, thank You for encouraging me to press on when
I want to quit and walk away. Give me strength and perseverance
in the great race of life until I cross the finish line and run
straight into Your waiting arms. In Jesus' name, amen.*

ADDITIONAL SCRIPTURE READING: PHILIPPIANS 4:10-19

44

Preparing for Baby

In my Father's house are many rooms; if it were not so, I would
have told you. I am going there to prepare a place for you.

JOHN 14:2

Carrie sat the brightly wrapped package on her bulging tummy and plucked the pastel bow from its lid. Everyone at the baby shower ooohed and aaahed as she held up an infant's pink terrycloth sleeper with tiny snaps and bootie feet. It was hard to believe that in just a few short weeks her first child would be filling that tiny outfit. Tears pooled in my eyes as I thought back to the wondrous days of anticipating the birth of *my* first child.

When a baby is snuggled in a mother's womb, he has no idea the commotion and excitement that surrounds his grand debut. The nursery is prepared down to the minutest detail with a strategically placed rocking chair waiting expectantly in the corner. A dancing mobile of elephants on parade is suspended midair above the shiny new crib. A music box ready to chime "It's a Small World" rests on a newly painted shelf. And a changing table with all the modern paraphernalia necessary to keep bottoms dry stands ready for work to begin. Bumper pads, blankets, and curtains all coordinate in a way that would make Martha Stewart proud. Then there's the painting and the sewing and the... well, the list is endless. No, a baby in the womb has no idea the preparations taking place or just how much love awaits his or her arrival.

And if I were to guess, we have no idea just how much preparation is taking place for our arrival in our eternal home. Jesus said, "In my Father's house are many rooms; if it were not so, I would have told you. I am going there to prepare a place for you" (John 14:2). God is preparing a room for you and for me. I imagine Him crafting each and every detail to perfection. And just as a baby has no idea how much love awaits him as he passes from the safe haven of his mother's womb and into her embracing arms, we have no idea just how much love awaits us as we pass from this temporary dwelling place and into our eternal home.

Today, imagine your heavenly Father's heart beating in anticipation for the day you will arrive to spend eternity with Him.

~~

Heavenly Father, I become so excited when I think about the home Jesus is preparing for me! What amazes me even more is the idea that You will be excited when I arrive! I can hardly wait! In Jesus' name, amen.

ADDITIONAL SCRIPTURE READING: JOHN 14:1-31

45

What Kind of a Friend Are You?

*Let us consider how we may spur one
another on toward love and good deeds.*

HEBREWS 10:24

It was an accidental experiment. Sometimes those are the best kind.

I had sent out an online devotion before my husband had a chance to proofread it. I have trouble finding my own errors because I know what I meant to say. (That is a lesson in itself. Just think on that a moment.) When I read the posted devotion, I was horrified. It was smattered with typos and mistakes. *Oh, well,* I thought as I humbly clicked "delete." *Grace, grace, grace.*

Then the comments from readers began to arrive.

"Check your spelling! Run a grammar check!" one woman wrote.

"Today's devotion meant so much to me," another shared. "Thank you for ministering to me."

Finally, one wrote, "Sharon, I just hate to see typos in your wonderful devotions. I know you are busy. Why don't you send them to me and I will proof them for you?"

In these e-mail responses, I saw three types of "friends."

- One woman simply pointed out my faults.
- One woman overlooked my faults and encouraged me in the ways I had blessed her.
- One woman encouraged me, acknowledged my errors, and then went one step further. She offered to help.

The Bible tells us, "As iron sharpens iron, so one man sharpens another" (Proverbs 27:17). The first woman didn't sharpen me at all. It was more like a stab. But now that I think about it, God did use her words to sharpen me. God showed me the critical type of woman I did *not* want to be and how *not* to use my words.

Interestingly, the Hebrew word for "mouth" used in the Old Testament can also be translated as "edge." Our words can have a sharp edge that wounds or heals, depending on how and when we use them. A knife in the hands of a skilled surgeon brings life, but a knife in the hands of a murderer brings death. Same instrument. Different use. As the writer of Proverbs said, "Death and life are in the power of the tongue" (Proverbs 18:21 NASB).

We can be one of those three types of friends. We can be the type who simply points out faults, the type who overlooks faults and focuses on the positives, or the type who praises someone's strengths and offers to help when there is a weakness.

What kind of a friend do you want to be?

God, help me to be a good friend—a friend who builds up rather than tears down, who encourages rather than discourages, and who fans the flames of a dream rather than puts out the fire. In Jesus' name, amen.

ADDITIONAL SCRIPTURE READING: 1 SAMUEL 20:1-42

46

When You Least Expect It

We are not unaware of [Satan's] schemes.

2 CORINTHIANS 2:11

On Tuesday morning, September 11, 2001, after I saw my son off to school and my husband off to work, I took a long walk through my neighborhood. The sky was crystal clear with a gentle breeze rustling the orange and yellows of the newly changing leaves. There was nothing special on my schedule—just the ordinary. But when I came back into the house, the day became anything but ordinary.

The phone was ringing. "Sharon, have you seen what has happened?" a friend asked with a tremble in her voice.

"No, what's wrong?" I asked.

"Turn on the television and see for yourself."

I watched in horror as the television played and replayed the airplanes crashing into the World Trade Center towers in New York City and the Pentagon in Washington, D.C. "Oh, God," I prayed, "we never saw it coming."

That's how the enemy always attacks, He seemed to say. *When you least expect it.*

My mind raced back to another day—December 31, 1999. It was the day the world braced itself for the potentially disastrous effects of Y2K. Families and businesses alike prepared for months for what might occur as the clock ticked past 11:59 p.m. Families stored up water, bought generators, and bolted safes in their home. Yes, we were ready.

Then, as the clock ticked over to the new millennium, we held our breaths, clasped our hands, and braced ourselves. What happened? Nothing. The new millennium came without incident. And yet, on an ordinary day, September 11, 2001, when we least expected it, an evil force attacked our country as never before in history.

Oh, dear friend, do you see the correlation? There is an enemy who seeks to kill, steal, and destroy (John 10:10). His name is Satan. He desires to destroy us just as the hijackers drove those airplanes into and toppled the twin towers. He's not very creative, but he is very effective, and he uses the same methods with us he's used since the beginning of time: lies. Our first line of defense is to be prepared. To be ready. To anticipate his attacks and be on the alert.

The devil has already been defeated by Jesus Christ's death and resurrection, but he still taunts and tempts God's children—dive-bombing into our lives on a regular basis. But when we hold up the shield of faith, his pitiful attempts will simply bounce off and *he* will be the one tumbling to the ground.

Today, let's put on the full armor of God and be alert to the enemy's tactics.

Dear God, keep me alert today. Help me to recognize the enemy's low growl when he comes prowling around my life. He has already lost the battle for my heart. Just help me to remind him. In Jesus' name, amen.

ADDITIONAL SCRIPTURE READING:
2 CORINTHIANS 10:1-5; LUKE 4:13

47

Putting on the Dog

Beware of practicing your righteousness before
men to be noticed by them; otherwise you have no
reward with your Father who is in heaven.

MATTHEW 6:1 NASB

Our golden retriever, Ginger, was never much of a watchdog. She mainly barked at women and young children. However, if a menacing-looking man approached the door, Ginger usually hid with her head under the car. She did have a particular dislike for the meter reader, but other than that she was a pretty useless protector. Most of the time when she did bark, her tail wagged at the same time, which made her a little less convincing. But occasionally she'd make the hair on her back stand up in an effort to look the part. I'm convinced it was only an act.

Even though I knew she was a cowardly fur ball, I had hoped that she was somewhat of a deterrent against unwanted solicitors and would-be robbers when we were away. Boy, was I disappointed when a neighbor informed me that Ginger only barked when we are at home! If we were gone, apparently she didn't even bother to get up, much less growl.

One spring we hired a painter to put a fresh coat of color on the outside of our house. He came while I wasn't home and had been working all day. That afternoon, when I pulled into the driveway, I was greeted with a tranquil picture of the painter standing on his ladder and Ginger lying peacefully at its feet. But when Ginger saw me, boy howdy, she jumped up and commenced to bark at her new friend the painter like there was no tomorrow!

"What's she doing?" he asked. "Why's she barking? That's the first peep I've heard from her all day."

Ah, her master was home. Time to get to work. Time to protect the castle.

Her entire life, Ginger did her job of protecting the house only when she thought we were watching. She made me think about my actions. Do I perform differently when someone's watching?

The truth is, our Master is always watching. He sees every move, hears every word, and perceives every thought. And if we live our lives trying to impress other people, we're simply barking up the wrong tree.

⌒

Dear Heavenly Father, I know You see everything
I do, hear every word I say, and sense every thought
I perceive. Forgive me when I perform well to please
mere people rather than You. In Jesus' name, amen.

ADDITIONAL SCRIPTURE READING:
MATTHEW 6:1-4; 1 THESSALONIANS 2:4-6

48

The Power of the Truth

You will know the truth,
and the truth will set you free.

JOHN 8:32

Hollywood was coming to town! The city was all abuzz as the movie cameras rolled in to tape *The Patriot,* starring Mel Gibson as Benjamin Martin. Several of my neighbors excitedly tried out to be stand-ins or extras for the film. One of my friends, Mike Moore, had a prosthetic leg due to cancer in his twenties and explained, "I'll be perfect for the battle scenes! I'm already missing a leg."

So off went the Moore family for the movie tryouts. In the end, the directors didn't choose Mike and his fake leg, but they did choose Mike's nine-year-old son, Michael. He was to be the stand-in for Benjamin Martin's son, Samuel. For months Michael wore his long hair with extensions, slipped on Italian knickers and knee-high stockings, and acted the part of an American colonial boy. He traveled to rural South Carolina where part of the movie was taped and received an education in the production of a film for the silver screen. Michael saw how producers and makeup artists made something appear as though it was real when it wasn't.

When the movie debuted, we were all anxious to see the scenes with little Michael.

The movie was a realistic reenactment of the horrors of the Revolutionary War. During one scene, Mel Gibson pummeled a British soldier and landed a hatchet square in the middle of his bloody forehead. I covered my eyes in horror. Michael didn't bat an eye. Why? He knew it wasn't real.

"That guy walked around the set with that hatchet in his head for three days," Michael explained. "We even ate lunch together, and he had that hatchet with fake blood glued to his face. It isn't real."

Then God reminded me that was the attitude I should have when

Satan tries to steal my faith and turn it into fear—when he whispers lies to cause worry and doubt. *That's not real!*

When we know God's truth, we can recognize the enemy's lies and put them back in the mental trash bin where they belong. Here's the battle plan: Realize the enemy's true identity, recognize the lies, reject the lies, and replace the lies with truth. It worked for Michael. It will work for you too! That's the power of the truth.

⌒

> *God, help me to recognize the lies of the evil one, reject*
> *the lies, and replace the lies with truth. I stand on the*
> *promises of Your Word and refuse to listen to anything*
> *contrary to Your truth. In Jesus' name, amen.*

ADDITIONAL SCRIPTURE READING: JOHN 8:31-36

49

The Work of Art

I praise you because I am fearfully and wonderfully made;
your works are wonderful, I know that full well.

PSALM 139:14

It was truly a work of art. Yes, one eye was much larger than the other, the nose resembled a giant squash, and the ears looked like saucers on the side of his head. But my kindergarten son's self-portrait unveiled on parents' night is a masterpiece I've treasured through the years.

As I looked at Steven's drawing, I noticed it had a striking resemblance to some works by the world-renowned Picasso. However, Picasso's paintings are worth millions of dollars, and my son's are valuable only to me. *I wonder why there is such a difference*, I mused. *The value must be based on the artist who created it.*

Ah, whispered God to my heart. *Now you're getting it.*

Then I began to realize that it is the same way with me. I have great value because of the Artist who created me. He meticulously created my inmost being, curiously knit me together in my mother's womb, and intricately wove me together with various colors and hues. Just as a masterpiece exists in the mind of the creator, God saw my unformed substance before the weaving even began.

Steven's masterpiece still hangs in my home today. And you and I are living works of art on display in God's universal gallery.

For you created my inmost being;
you knit me together in my mother's womb.
I praise you because I am fearfully and wonderfully made;
your works are wonderful,
I know that full well.
My frame was not hidden from you
when I was made in the secret place.
When I was woven together in the depths of the earth,

your eyes saw my unformed body.
All the days ordained for me
were written in your book
before one of them came to be.

PSALM 139:13-16

⌒

Dear God, I praise You because I am fearfully and
wonderfully made. Forgive me for complaining about
Your handiwork. I am truly a masterpiece of Your creative
genius...I know this full well. In Jesus' name, amen.

ADDITIONAL SCRIPTURE READING: PSALM 139:1-18

50

Lost and Found

The Son of Man came to seek and to save what was lost.

LUKE 19:10

I don't know if I've ever seen a little boy so excited! Steven was seven years old and we were headed for Disney World! It was his first time on an airplane, his first time sleeping in a hotel, and his first time to see Mickey Mouse in person.

My video camera was fully charged and poised to capture those precious memories. But the video didn't start out as I had planned. As it begins, we're in a welcome center where children are running around, climbing on various objects, crawling through tunnels, and swinging from monkey bars. As the movie continues, I see my husband running toward the camera, his face growing larger and larger until it fills the frame.

"Where's Steven?" he cries. "I can't find him anywhere!"

Then the screen goes blank.

What a way to start our vacation! Steven had wandered away, climbed into one of those tunnels, and had yet to emerge. Of course we panicked. Who wants to lose their kid at Disney World? Of course we found him. He had no idea he was even lost.

Ah, did that last sentence give you pause? *He had no idea he was even lost...*

Even as I wrote it, God quickly reminded me that I was in the same situation. I had no idea I was lost, but my heavenly Father found me.

When God created Adam and Eve, He placed them in a garden much more exciting than Disney World. In the Garden of Eden all their needs were cared for and all their desires were fulfilled. But Satan came along and convinced Eve that God was holding out on her. There was more. If she would simply disobey God, eat of the forbidden fruit, she could be like God.

Eve bought the lie and disobeyed. Then she convinced her husband to disobey with her. And...well, we know the rest of the story. They were lost.

Suddenly the scene changes. We see fear, shame, and doubt as they hide from God. God walks through the garden and doesn't see His children. Then He asked the first question that is recorded in the Bible... "Where are you?"

Friend, it was the first question in the Bible and it runs like a scarlet thread all the way to the end of Revelation. "Where are you?"

Steven was lost and didn't even know it, but his daddy found him.

We were lost and didn't even know it, but our heavenly Father found us.

So that's the question I want to leave with you today. Where are you? How's your relationship with God? No matter what you've done, no matter how far you've strayed from His perfect plan for your life, He is always in pursuit of you. All you have to do is come out from hiding and say, "Here I am, Lord."

Heavenly Father, thank You for rescuing me when I was lost and didn't even know it. You are the hero in the grand drama of my life, and I will be eternally grateful. In Jesus' name, amen.

ADDITIONAL SCRIPTURE READING: LUKE 19:1-10; LUKE 15:1-7

51

Three Squirrels

*He who began a good work in you will carry it on
to completion until the day of Christ Jesus.*

PHILIPPIANS 1:6

The squirrels were driving me mad! As soon as I'd fill up the bird feeder, three squirrels would come along and empty it out. They would hang upside down by one grubby paw while seemingly waving at me with the other. And for some reason there were always three of them. I tried various contraptions to keep them at bay, but they always figured out a way to overcome the obstacles. They would find a way over it, under it, around it, or even sit on it.

Finally I resorted to a squirrel cage to capture the furry varmints and release them in a distant field. I told my idea to my skeptical husband and explained, "All I have to do is put some food—birdseed, of course—in the cage and leave the door open. When the squirrel creeps into the cage, the door closes and traps the fellow inside. It will not hurt him at all. Then I can take the little darling out into the country where he can live long and prosper. It will be easy."

Steve said, "I'll remember those words in a few weeks, especially the last one, 'easy.'"

The first day was met with great success. Thirty minutes after the bait was set, I had a conquest. As I approached the caged animal, I wasn't sure who was more afraid, the squirrel or me. I had actually not been up close and personal with a squirrel before, and from the squirrel's reaction to me, he had never been up close and personal with a human before. I donned thick gloves, lifted the cage, and took my furry friend to his new home out in the country. When I opened the cage door to let him out, he never looked back but shot out of the cage like a speeding bullet. By the end of the day, I had made three trips to the country, safely depositing all three of the squirrels. That night, sleep was sweet.

You can imagine my horror when I arose the next morning to look out at the bird feeder and see squirrels—*three* squirrels. Were these the same squirrels? A call to the veterinarian assured me that the squirrels on Day Two were not the same squirrels from Day One. He said that as long as they had water and food where they were, they would just stay put. So I repeated the previous day's three journeys to the country with my three little friends.

On the third morning of the battle, I was almost afraid to look. Peeping out from behind the curtain, what did I see? You guessed it. Three squirrels at the feeder. I set the trap, caught the squirrels, and then transported the squirrels. I was not happy.

Day Four, same story. Three squirrels. Three trips to the country. Only this time, after taking the squirrels to the country, I drove directly back to my neighbor's house to return the cage. She was expecting me.

It seemed that when I captured and removed the three squirrels, that opened the way for more to come and fill the vacancy.

The critters reminded me of the squirrelly attitudes, behaviors, and thoughts I've tried to eradicate in my own life. It seems that just as soon as I have victory in one area, God shows me another that needs to be captured as well.

I gave up on the squirrels, but I'm so thankful God will never give up on me!

Ask God what attitudes or behaviors in your own life need capturing. He'll show you.

⌐

*Dear God, thank You for Your patience with my
squirrelly behavior and nutty attitude. And thank You
for not giving up on me. In Jesus' name, amen.*

ADDITIONAL SCRIPTURE READING: PHILIPPIANS 1:3-11

52

No More Begging

Now if we are children, then we are heirs—
heirs of God and co-heirs with Christ.

ROMANS 8:17

Dave and Bonnie read about the overcrowded orphanages in Eastern Europe, and God stirred their hearts to adopt not one, two, or three, but four little boys. Foreign adoptions are very costly, but the Jacobs had been richly blessed and money was not a problem. After eleven months and miles of red tape, the adoption process was complete and the couple traveled across the ocean to gather their new family.

The flight home was a grueling ten hours, so when they arrived at the Atlanta airport for a two-hour layover, Dave and Bonnie let their rambunctious new sons run around the terminal to work out some of their little boy energy. Of course, they never let their sons out of their sight. After a short while, Dave noticed that one of the boys was watching a man drinking at a water fountain. Even though the child could not speak English, he seemed to be making hand motions and using body language to communicate. Dave watched as the man reached in his pocket, pulled out a dollar bill, and handed it to his son.

Dave ran over to the man and exclaimed, "What are you doing?"

"Well, I could tell this little boy couldn't speak English, but I could also tell he was begging. So I gave him a dollar."

Dave looked in his new son's pocket, and he had ten $1 bills!

Oh, how I see myself in that little boy's eyes. Adopted by the King of kings and yet still begging for others to fill me up. The little boy had no idea of the riches that came with his adoption. His every need would be met by his new daddy. And even though he was now part of a family with great wealth, he continued to beg for what was freely his.

When we come to Christ, the Bible tells us we are adopted into God's family as co-heirs with Christ. That means we get what Jesus gets. And yet we still go through life begging for other people to meet our emotional, spiritual, and physical needs. We beg for approval from coworkers and family members. We long for affection from friends and spouses. We purchase more and more *things,* as if *things* will somehow satisfy our longings. However, our heavenly Father owns the cattle on a thousand hills, and we never need to beg for what God wants to freely give.

Today, let's make sure to live like children of the King!

Heavenly Father, forgive me for living like a spiritual pauper when I am a child of the King. Thank You for adopting me into Your family and making me a co-heir with Your Son, Jesus. In Jesus' name, amen.

ADDITIONAL SCRIPTURE READING: ROMANS 8:1-17

53

Be Careful What You Pray

*In the morning I lay my requests
before you and wait in expectation.*

Psalm 5:3

Lord, we thank You for this beautiful summer day. I pray Steven and Sharon will see and experience Your creation in a new and fresh way today. Amen."

Summer is a wonderful time of year to experience God's creation, with new flowers stretching through their brown blankets of soil and animals unfurling from the darkened holes of winter. Steve's prayer for God to bless our day before he scurried off to work one balmy summer morning was most welcomed. As soon as he walked out the door, it seemed God got busy answering his prayer.

Much to my horror and my son's delight, we have a zoo of color-changing, eyeball-blinking, tongue-hurling lizards around the perimeter of our house and yard. I decided years ago that I did not like anything that looked you in the eye and stuck out its tongue. However, if the lizards remained outside where God created them to be, we could coexist splendidly.

But on this particular day, a miniature reptile decided to do an inspection tour of my kitchen. With a swat of the broom, his tail detached while the remainder of his scaly body scurried across the room. More swats ensued, and the lizard was finally swept outside.

Later that afternoon, I glanced out of the porch window to see a huge black snake basking in the summer sun by the sidewalk steps. His erect head scoped out the area like a submarine periscope on the open sea. A frantic call to a neighbor who was home for lunch brought hoes, shovels, and excited neighborhood boys to witness the snake's demise.

Emotionally weary from "seeing God's creation in a new and fresh way," I plopped down at the dinner table and stared out onto our peaceful lawn. "What's that hopping across the yard?" I asked.

Steve stood up and watched as an overly stuffed field mouse bounded toward the area where our dog, Ginger, was sleeping. Alert to the scent, Ginger went into action. She looked as if she was not sure exactly what was expected of her, but she knew it was something. I thought to myself, *Where's a snake when you need it?* Ginger pawed and terrorized this misplaced rodent. By the time Steve put the mouse out of his misery, our dinner was ruined.

My goodness. One simple prayer, and what did we get? A lizard with a detachable tail in my kitchen, a slithering snake on my side steps, and a hopping field mouse for dinner entertainment. Psalm 5:3 says, "In the morning I will order my prayer to You and eagerly watch" (NASB).

Exhausted, I turned to Steve and said, "Next time you pray for God to reveal His creation in a 'new and fresh way,' could you please be more specific?"

I hope this devotion made you smile. But the truth is, God does invite us to be specific in our requests. Go ahead. Tell Him what's on your heart. He's listening.

Heavenly Father, thank You for answering my prayers, even when You do it in a way that I wasn't expecting. In Jesus' name, amen.

ADDITIONAL SCRIPTURE READING:
PSALM 5:1-3; MATTHEW 7:7-11

54

The Stairway

You are no longer a slave, but a son; and since you are a son,
God has made you also an heir.

GALATIANS 4:7

Imagine you have just been told that you have inherited a multi-level mansion equipped with every conceivable treasure. You run up the curving brick sidewalk, throw open the massive oak doors, and excitedly run from room to room hardly believing the good fortune bequeathed to you! However, what you discover are not the surroundings fit for a queen that you expected, but sensible chambers, adequately furnished and sparsely decorated.

In the foyer a beautifully carved winding staircase, adorned with plush crimson carpet, beckons you to climb to the next level. You consider the steps, look back over your shoulder, and decide, "Hey, the lower level's enough for me. Besides, I'm afraid of heights. I'll just stay down here where it's safe."

Unbeknownst to you, the upper levels house all the treasures intended to become your inheritance, and you're standing in the servants' quarters. Upstairs await a golden gilded ballroom, a chandeliered dining hall, four-poster beds with down-filled mattresses, a safe filled with enough gold and silver to last a lifetime, and a jewelry box brimming with family heirlooms. All that stands between you and these treasures is the staircase. What keeps you on ground level? Contentment with mediocrity? Fear of the unknown?

We all have an inheritance from our Father. The Bible tells us we have been blessed with every spiritual blessing in the heavenly realm. But oftentimes we spend our days in the servants' quarters, never climbing the stairs to where the true riches are stored. It is as though we win the spiritual lottery but forget to cash the check. Instead, we put it in a frame and place it on a shelf for display in our ragtag lives. "Look what I've got!" we say as we scrounge about in our miserable existence. "If you accept Jesus, you can have one of these too!"

Oh, dear. No wonder so few are interested in what we have to offer.

Here's an idea. Let's approach the stairs and climb—no, run!—to find the spiritual treasures that are ours in Christ Jesus. Let's throw open the doors to our spiritual inheritance and enjoy God as never before. And when we do, we'll hear footsteps of a hungry world following behind.

Listen closely. He's calling you to discover and enjoy the inheritance waiting for you.

Dear Father, I confess I have stayed in the servants' quarters of life way too long. Give me the courage to run up the stairs of opportunity and open the doors to all the riches You have waiting for me there. In Jesus' name, amen.

ADDITIONAL SCRIPTURE READING: GALATIANS 3:26–4:7

55

It's a Small, Small World

We fix our eyes not on what is seen, but on what is unseen.
For what is seen is temporary, but what is unseen is eternal.

2 CORINTHIANS 4:18

"Everything was so small," my husband explained as he replayed his visit to his childhood home. "Nothing was like I remembered."

Steve woke one Saturday morning with a nostalgic urge to revisit the small North Carolina town where he spent the first eight years of his childhood. At family gatherings, he and his brother recounted endless stories of playing kick-the-can and baseball in their front yard, which was "at least the size of a football field." The long hardwood hallways in their spacious home where they slid sock-footed were "at least as long as a bowling alley." They told tales of spacious grassy hills where they rolled their bodies from top to bottom, itching and laughing all the way.

So the little boy in Steve hopped on his horse (a gold Honda Accord) and galloped off to look for buried treasure. With map in hand, he located the big *X* where those wonderful memories were made. He pulled up to the address, blinked in unbelief, and checked the map again.

"This can't be it," he mused. What he saw was not a spacious home, but a tiny square bungalow. The yard "the size of a football field" was in reality the size of a baseball infield with the house sitting on the pitcher's mound. And the "rolling hills" were no more than two consecutive humps.

Steve spent the day driving from one landmark to another, and each time reality clashed with memory. "Everything is so small," he repeated time and time again. The visit was a startling shock to Steve's mental scrapbook, and part of him wished he'd left the memories undisturbed. The happy memories of two rambunctious boys sliding through hallways and rolling down hills were still etched in his mind. But the halls became shorter and the hills became smaller.

As I listened to my husband tell of his adventure, I realized this is how I imagine most people in heaven will react to our simple lives on earth. We tend to think our world is so grand…and don't get me wrong, it certainly is. But majestic sunsets, star-filled nights, and vast oceans only hint at God's creative genius. This earth cannot even compare to the glorious home waiting those who believe. One day we will be face-to-face with God, basking in His eternal light, lingering in His limitless love, and feasting on His boundless goodness. When we get there, we'll never want to go back to earth.

Bask in these words today:

> Then I saw a new heaven and a new earth, for the first heaven and the first earth had passed away, and there was no longer any sea. I saw the Holy City, the new Jerusalem, coming down out of heaven from God, prepared as a bride beautifully dressed for her husband. And I heard a loud voice from the throne saying, "Now the dwelling of God is with men, and he will live with them. They will be his people, and God himself will be with them and be their God. He will wipe every tear from their eyes. There will be no more death or mourning or crying or pain, for the old order of things has passed away" (Revelation 21:1-4).

Heavenly Father, I love this life You have given me, but I also look forward to the day when I will be in Your presence for all eternity. I know that the goodness in this life is only a small taste of the glorious adventure that is yet to come. In Jesus' name, amen.

ADDITIONAL SCRIPTURE READING: 2 CORINTHIANS 4:1-18

56

The Right Credentials

In him and through faith in him we may approach
God with freedom and confidence.

EPHESIANS 3:12

Y ou're not supposed to be here! Where are your credentials? You're
in a lot of trouble."

I can still remember the security guard's words as he pointed a
gnarly finger in my face.

Patsy Clairmont has been an inspiration to me ever since the time
I first read *God Uses Cracked Pots*. We were discussing my first book on
the telephone one day and trying to set up a time to meet face-to-face
when she came to speak at the Women of Faith Conference at the coliseum in my hometown of Charlotte.

"Patsy, I'd love to spend some time with you before the conference,
but I don't have a backstage pass. I won't have access to where you'll
be," I explained.

"No problem," Patsy answered. "Just go to my book table and tell
my son who you are. He'll bring you to me."

The day of the conference arrived and I swam through a sea of
women to reach Patsy's crowded book table. After making the proper
introductions with Patsy's son, we were off to find his mom. First we
passed through heavy mahogany double doors that led to an area called
the Crown Room, a place for the VIPs who attended professional basketball games at the coliseum. Then we hopped on an elevator that
took us to where another group of VIPs (Very Inspiring People) were
tucked away.

As I stepped into the elevator, a stern security guard pointed his
finger in my face and pronounced, "You're not supposed to be here!
Where are your credentials? You're in a lot of trouble."

He whipped out his walkie-talkie and was not afraid to use it.
Before I could force one word out of my dry mouth, Patsy's son stepped

forward, showed the guard his backstage pass, and gallantly stated, "I'm one of the speakers' sons. I have a pass. She's with me."

"That's right, mister," I agreed once I found my tongue. "He's Patsy Clairmont's son, and I'm with him."

"Oh, okay then." And the guard was off to seek and find other dangerous Christian women like myself who were attending the conference.

I visited with Patsy and then returned to enjoy the conference. It was certainly an inspiring infusion of power-packed excitement. But perhaps the greatest lesson I learned that day was on the elevator ride.

See, one day I'm going to leave this earth and pass through a crown room of God's making…a room meant for only the VIPs who have their names written in the Lamb's book of life. And I imagine someone will be hiding in the wings to check out people's credentials. The Bible calls him the accuser of the brethren, who accuses them day and night (Revelation 12:10). I can just picture him now, jumping out to block my way and pointing his own gnarly finger in my face.

"What are you doing here?" he might say. "You don't belong here. Where's your heavenly pass? What are your credentials?"

Then just as Patsy's son stepped forward, God's Son, Jesus Christ, will step forward on my behalf. "I'm Jesus Christ. I'm God's Son. She's with me, and I'm all the credentials she needs."

And, friend, if you know Jesus Christ as Savior and Lord, then He's all the credentials you'll need as well. I'll see you there!

Dear God, thank You that I acquired all the credentials I need for eternal life when I accepted Jesus Christ as my Savior and made Him Lord of my life! In Jesus' name, amen.

ADDITIONAL SCRIPTURE READING: EPHESIANS 1:1-12

57

Inducted

It is by grace you have been saved, through faith—
and this not from yourselves, it is the gift of God—
not by works, so that no one can boast.

EPHESIANS 2:8

Sharon. This is Mary Ruth. I am so excited. Let me read you this letter that Alexander just received from his school today. It says, 'Dear Alexander, we are pleased to inform you that because of your high grade point average and excellent exhibition of character, you have been inducted into the National Honor Society.' Isn't that great?"

Mary Ruth was so proud when she received this important letter in the mail and couldn't wait to read it to me over the phone. We rejoiced together over Alex's accomplishment.

But then, three months later, she called me back with a different letter.

"Sharon, this is Mary Ruth. You won't believe what was in the mail today. We got another letter from school, and it reads, 'Dear Alexander, we are sorry to inform you that because your grade point average has fallen below the necessary requirements, you are no longer eligible for the National Honor Society.'"

In other words, Alex was *inducted*, but then he got *deducted*. This is not the kind of letter a parent wants to open, but it made me think about how glad I am that since I have been inducted into the family of God, I never have to worry about the possibility of being deducted because I haven't kept up my spiritual grade point average. Ephesians 2:8-9 says, "By grace you have been saved through faith; and that not of yourselves, it is the gift of God; not as a result of works, so that no one may boast" (NASB).

I have not been initiated into the kingdom of God because of anything I've done. It is a gift. And it's a good thing too, because I could never make the grades good enough to get in, and I could never maintain the grades to stay in. The good news is that Jesus has already done it for me. He took the test. He passed with flying colors. And I reap the benefits.

I imagine a letter like this one coming to my house. "Dear Sharon, congratulations. Because of the shed blood of Jesus Christ, His call on your life, and your submissive heart, you have been inducted into the Heavenly Honor Society. All the requirements have been met, once and for all. Signed with love, Jehovah."

Are you trying to earn your way to heaven, or are you resting in the truth that Jesus has already done it for you? Today, let's thank God for inviting us to spend eternity with Him. Let's praise Him that while we could never be good enough, smart enough, or pure enough, Jesus Christ's sacrifice has done it for us.

Dear God, thank You for providing a way for me to be cleansed of my sin and welcomed into Your kingdom. Thank You that just as I didn't have to work to earn it, I don't have to work to keep it. I rest in the assurance of my eternal salvation. In Jesus' name, amen.

ADDITIONAL SCRIPTURE READING: EPHESIANS 2:1-10

58

Rearview Living

One thing I do: Forgetting what is behind and straining toward
what is ahead, I press on toward the goal to win the prize
for which God has called me heavenward in Christ Jesus.

PHILIPPIANS 3:13-14

I turned the steering wheel a bit to the right, a bit to the left, and then back to the right again. *Why am I having trouble backing down this straight driveway?*

I sat in my car, dreading the drive down my friend Brenda's driveway. The concrete path resembled a ski slope, and I was parked at the top, the nose of my car pointing heavenward and the rear to the street below.

Normally, I would have rolled down my window and poked my head out to look where I was going. But today the clouds had decided to empty their entire contents all at once, and I was dependent on my rearview mirror.

The driveway was a straight shot down, but as I looked into the mirror and inched my way backward, I found myself turning a little to the left, then a little to the right, and finally a little back to the left again. Twice I left the pavement and my tires visited the wet grass.

Why is this so hard? I moaned to no one in particular.

Then an unexpected stirring answered. *You're having trouble because cars aren't meant to be driven backward...and neither are you.*

Suddenly I saw more in my rearview mirror than the steep driveway behind me. I began to see the reason many of us have trouble driving down the road of life—we spend too much time looking in the rearview mirror and not enough time looking straight ahead.

In our spiritual journey, it is beneficial to look back to see where we've been, how far God has brought us, and what He has done in our lives. But if we drive through life spending too much time looking in the rearview mirror at past mistakes, abuses, and failures with cries of "if only," we're in for a lot of wrecks.

There is a warning etched onto the glass of my car's side mirror, "Objects in mirror are closer than they appear." In other words, looking in the rearview mirror will distort your visual perception. It is hard to look at the past and keep the reality of the situation true to what it really was. One has a tendency to either romanticize life and forget the negative or to take traumatic situations and accentuate the negative until all positive memories are lost. Focusing on the past can lead to a distorted view of reality.

So what's the answer? I do need to look back in order to see what the Lord has done for me and to remind myself of His faithfulness. But I don't need to go through life looking backward to find someone to blame each time I veer off the road. Rearview mirrors are helpful and necessary, but if we choose to drive through life looking backward instead of forward, we're in for a rough ride.

Today, let's decide to spend less time looking at where we've been and more time looking at where God wants us to go! And while we're looking ahead, let's listen to that still, small voice telling us which way to go.

As the prophet Isaiah assured us: "Whether you turn to the right or to the left, your ears will hear a voice behind you, saying, 'This is the way; walk in it'" (Isaiah 30:21).

Dear Lord, today I resist the temptation to say "what if" or "if only." I look forward to what the future holds and keep my eyes fixed on You. In Jesus' name, amen.

ADDITIONAL SCRIPTURE READING: PHILIPPIANS 3:7–4:1

59

Setting Dreams Afloat

*Now to him who is able to do immeasurably
more than all we ask or imagine...to him be glory.*

Ephesians 3:20-21

I suddenly felt like Moses' big sister hiding in the bulrushes, waiting to see if someone was going to pull my "baby" from the crocodile-infested Nile. This may tend toward the dramatic, but it describes how I felt when I went to the Christian Book Association convention to present my first manuscript to various publishers many years ago. I wondered if anyone would rescue my "baby" from the piles of manuscripts floating around the convention floor. I wondered if anyone would think my "baby" beautiful and adopt it into their publishing family.

As I prayed, God reminded me of Moses' mother. The first two chapters of the book of Exodus tell us that Pharaoh had decided the Hebrews were growing too numerous. He feared these slaves would eventually become so strong in number and strength that they might revolt and try to take over Egypt. So he issued a decree that all the newborn male Hebrew babies be thrown into the Nile River.

Jochebed was a very resourceful woman. When her baby boy was born, she hid him for as long as she could, and then she came up with a plan. She fashioned a tiny ark of papyrus leaves and covered it with tar and pitch. Then she placed Moses in the basket and set it afloat in the crocodile-infested Nile. While she stayed home to pray, the baby's big sister hid in the bushes to see if anyone would rescue her brother.

Who should come along but the one person in the kingdom who could do whatever she wished...Pharaoh's daughter. She saw the basket among the reeds and sent her slave girl to retrieve it. When she pulled back the blanket, there lay sweet little tear-drenched Moses.

"This is one of the Hebrew babies," she said.

On cue, Miriam shot out from the bushes and offered up a

suggestion. "I know where you can get a wet nurse for the baby! Shall I go and get her?"

"Yes, go," the princess answered.

Moses was saved and Jochebed nursed her son for at least two years. Then at the appropriate time, she placed him in the arms of the princess to be raised with all the best Egypt had to offer. What a dream come true! God answered her prayers exceedingly abundantly above all that she could have ever asked or thought (Ephesians 3:20).

So I followed Jochebed's lead. I placed my hopes and dreams in a basket and set it adrift among the sea of editors. Then I waited anxiously to see if anyone would think it beautiful. They did.

Dreams are not meant to be clutched close to our breasts and held in fear. They are meant to be released in prayer. It may be frightening, those first steps of faith, but just as a bird was not made for the nest nor a ship for the harbor, our dreams are not meant to be kept tucked away for safekeeping. They are meant to set sail on the ocean of opportunity for horizons unknown.

But it takes trust to cut anchor and raise the sails. We have to trust God with our hopes and dreams. And no matter what happens when we set them afloat or in flight, we can be assured God has a plan for each of us. "No eye has seen, no ear has heard, no mind has conceived what God has prepared for those who love him" (1 Corinthians 2:9). And that, my friend, includes you!

Moses' mother had a simple dream—that her son would be delivered. God had a bigger dream—that Moses would be a deliverer. Place your dreams into God's hands and watch Him accomplish more than you ever imagined.

⌐⌐

Dear Lord, I give You my hopes and dreams. Give me the wisdom to know when I need to walk through an open door and wisdom to stop knocking when one remains closed. In Jesus' name, amen.

ADDITIONAL SCRIPTURE READING: EXODUS 2:1-10

60

Overheating Again

An angry man stirs up dissension,
and a hot-tempered one commits many sins.

PROVERBS 29:22

I don't know much about cars, but I have learned a valuable lesson. When the little red needle that fluctuates between *C* and *H* points to *H*, you need to stop right away.

We had a station wagon that had a hot temper. So many things went wrong with that car that the repair man began to recognize my voice when I called the shop. One day when I glanced down at the gauges with all the little red needles that tell you insignificant information, such as how fast you are going and how much fuel is in the tank, I noticed a needle pointing to a big *H*. I assumed that meant the car was hot. Well, it was August, and frankly I had been hot all day. So I figured, "What's the big deal?" In any case, I thought it would be a good idea to mosey on down to the dealership, ten miles away, and get them to check it out. Big mistake.

A few miles later, smoke started pouring out from under the hood. But did I stop? No, indeedy! I just kept going, trying to make it to the repair shop before closing time. Finally, right in the middle of an intersection, the little engine that could decided that it couldn't any longer, and it died. Thus began my first lesson on just how important that little *H* was on my control panel.

After my car was towed to the shop, I had an enlightening conversation with the mechanic. "Mrs. Jaynes, do you see that needle that is pointing to *H*? That means that the engine is runnin' hot. When you see that, you have to stop right away, but since you kept goin', you burned up your engine. It's a goner. You'll have to get a new one."

"That sounds expensive," I moaned.

"It'll be about four thousand dollars," he answered while continuing to poke around under the hood.

Four thousand dollars! And all because I didn't stop the car when it was overheated. All because I didn't heed the warning signs.

Cars aren't the only things that overheat. I can think of more than a few times when I have overheated myself. There have been times when my coolant has leaked out all over the road or times when I have run out of the oil of gladness. There have been times when I've wanted to bite somebody's head off or set the record straight once and for all. Being stuck in traffic when I'm already 15 minutes late to an appointment, having to go back to school because my son forgot a book in a subject that he has a test on the next day, discovering that someone left a blue ink pen in his pocket that has gone through the washing machine, all make my engine overheat.

When I start to heat up, I have a tendency to stew a little bit, simmer over the situation, and then pour out steam on whoever happens to be in earshot. Ephesians 4:26 reads, "If you are angry, don't sin by nursing your grudge" (TLB). I'd lump stewing and nursing in the same category. Both should be a warning signal that the temperature needle is getting a little off center and too close to that big red *H*. But before I blow a gasket and my coolant leaks out, I need to pull over and let my engine cool down.

How about you? Do you know the warning signals that indicate your engine is about to overheat? My suggestion is to pull off the road immediately and let the engine cool down. And while you're at it, pray that God will take a look under your hood and see what the cause of the problem really is.

Listen closely. He'll tell you.

Lord, You are the Master Mechanic in my life. Who else is better at fixing the problems under my hood than the One who made this piece of work called "me" in the first place? Help me to listen to Your warning signals when I'm about to overheat and to stop immediately to cool down and pray. In Jesus' name, amen.

ADDITIONAL SCRIPTURE READING:
EPHESIANS 4:26-27; JAMES 1:20

61

Humbled and Amazed

Let us stop passing judgment on one another.

ROMANS 14:13

You can learn a lot about human nature while watching people on the beach. Teenage girls position themselves strategically to be noticed by muscular young men strutting down the sandy runway. Dads pass footballs to admiring sons who were delighted to have some time to spend with their heroes. Moms in skirted swimsuits look at bikini-clad teens in disgust while secretly lamenting bygone days of flat tummies and slender thighs. Little tots squeal in delight at the sudden freedom to play in the sand with no one telling them to stay out of the dirt. Tiny feet are in constant motion like little windup toys running from mom to the water, and back to mom again. Have you ever noticed that no child under the age of four walks at the beach? It's a gallop, a skip, or a sprint. But it's never a walk.

One beautiful summer day, I was casually reclining in my lounge chair people-watching. I noticed a family on my immediate right. The small-framed mother was kneeling by her adult son and wiping the sand off of his feet with a towel. Then she carefully slipped his shoes on his clean feet. The young man was casually reading a book, never looking up, as his subservient mother waited on him.

Humph, I thought to myself. *Why is that mother waiting on her son hand and foot? Let him wipe his own feet!* I closed my eyes to laze in the sun, and soon the image of this subservient mom drifted away.

Later that evening, cleaned and refreshed from the day's salt and sand, we crowded into the hotel elevator in search of dinner. Who should be sharing the elevator with us but the family with the feet-wiping mother? We reached the ground floor, and the men parted to let her pass. Then her son awkwardly followed behind. His legs were fitted with metal braces. His arms were cuffed with metal crutches. He awkwardly swung the crutches forward and propelled his lower body toward the door.

The elevator emptied...except for me. Mirrored walls captured my pained expression as shame filled my heart. Subservient indeed! Now a whole new list of words describing this mother flooded my mind: loving, tender, caring, pained, sacrificial, and brave.

"Lord, forgive me," I prayed.

You can learn a lot about human nature by watching people on the beach. That day, I learned a lot about my own.

God, I am so quick to jump to conclusions. Forgive my judgmental attitude. Help me always to remember that only You know what is going on in another person's heart and life. In Jesus' name, amen.

ADDITIONAL SCRIPTURE READING:
ROMANS 14:1-13; MATTHEW 7:1-5

62

Lucky to Have a Son like You

Sons are a heritage from the LORD, *children a reward from him.*
PSALM 127:3

I don't find amusement parks very amusing. The lines are long, the rides make me queasy, the asphalt is hot, and the food is overpriced. But summer was just about over, and I thought my ten-year-old son might enjoy one last fling. Once again I paid good money to be spun in circles, gyrated up and down, and jerked to sudden stops from 60 miles per hour. I was feeling quite the martyr as I made this personal sacrifice. I certainly hoped Steven appreciated what a great mom he had.

Being unsure he had come to this conclusion, I thought I should bring it to his attention. Just before being hurled down a roller coaster track and into a pool of water at the end, I leaned forward and was just about to say, "Steven, you are so lucky to have a mom like me to bring you to a place like this." But before the words escaped my lips, the Holy Spirit stopped me.

Is that what you really want to say? Would those words make Steven feel "lucky" to have a mom like you or would they make him feel guilty, as though he owed you something?

So, instead of uttering my initial thought, I wrapped my arms around my precious young son and said, "Steven, *I* am so lucky to have a son like you I can bring to a place like this!"

With those words, a dimpled smile spread across his face, and I was thankful for the splash of the watery roller coaster that disguised the tears streaming down my face.

Perhaps you have some old tapes from your past that you tend to replay with your children. Did your mother make comments that caused you to feel guilty or as if you were indebted to her for the care she gave? Perhaps she still does. Many moms could be travel agents for guilt trips. But is that how you want to be remembered?

140

I had success with my words that day at the amusement park, but not every day has been a banner day. Let's pray that God will help us be women who use our words to build others up rather than tear them down, to encourage rather than discourage, and to spur others on rather than hold them back. Let's remember that our words become the mirrors in which others see themselves.

Dear Lord, I pray that the Holy Spirit will be the gatekeeper of my mouth today. I pray that the words I speak will help others see themselves as You see them... as dearly loved children of God. In Jesus' name, amen.

ADDITIONAL SCRIPTURE READING:
PSALM 127:1-5; PROVERBS 18:20-21

63

Mona Lisa

The king is enthralled by your beauty.

PSALM 45:11

Some say she's one of the most beautiful women in the world, but to me she looked rather ordinary.

One summer I visited the Louvre art museum in Paris. At the end of a long corridor lined with famous paintings, a crowd gathered to capture a glimpse of the famous *Mona Lisa*. Men and women jostled for position just to get a peek. Honestly, to me she looked rather plain. I didn't understand why she was so popular...until I heard the tour guide explain her history.

No one is really sure of *Mona Lisa's* true identity, but many think her to be Francesco di Bartolomeo di Zanobi del Giocondo's third wife, Lisa di Antonio Maria di Gherardini. (Try remembering those names! No wonder most people just say, "We don't know who she is.") She was painted by Leonardo da Vinci between 1503 and 1507. The painting moved from King Francis I's castle, to Fontainebleau, to Paris, to Versailles, to Napoleon's estate, and ended up in the Louvre.

However, on August 21, 1911, *Mona Lisa* was stolen by an Italian thief. During that time, the Parisians placed another painting in *Mona Lisa's* spot, but the citizens missed her terribly. Two years later, she emerged in Florence and was returned to Paris. Today, she remains in the Louvre behind a bulletproof glass.

Why is she so loved? Because once she was lost, but now she is found. She was stolen from her place of honor, but someone found her, paid the price for her, and put her back in her rightful place. No wonder she's smiling.

So it is with us, dear friend. Once we were lost, but now we've been found and placed back in our rightful place as children of the King. Psalm 45:11 says, "The king is enthralled by your beauty." That means He is captivated, fascinated, enraptured, smitten, spellbound, and taken with you. And that's why we should be smiling too.

～

Dear God, thank You for rescuing me from the thief
and his domain of darkness and placing me in the
kingdom of light with Your Son. You have given me
so much to smile about. In Jesus' name, amen.

ADDITIONAL SCRIPTURE READING:
ZEPHANIAH 3:17; LUKE 15:3-10

64

Boundary Line

The boundary lines have fallen for me in pleasant places;
surely I have a delightful inheritance.

PSALM 16:6

She was at it again. Our eccentric neighbor was in our yard trimming our bushes and pruning our trees. When we built our home, we were blessed with a big backyard 150 feet from our backdoor neighbor's lot line. The "Smiths" had lived in their home about 14 years before we came along and had landscaped the back third of our lot as if it were their own. They cleared the back part of the woods, planted a beautiful stand of ivy, and clustered a settee constructed of logs underneath a shade tree. A gravel extension of their driveway with an adjoining basketball court of sorts stood in the back corner.

It was all very lovely, but after we purchased the land, all of that was officially on our property. The surveyor's tape demarcating the property line went smack-dab down the middle of their driveway. What would we say? How would we get up the nerve to tell them that part of their driveway was in our yard? This was not a good way to start a neighborly relationship. We decided to let it go. We didn't need that part of the yard anyway.

We had a wonderful relationship with Mr. Smith, but Mrs. Smith never got used to us being there. She acted as though we were imposing on her annex. And over the years the boundary line grew a bit fuzzy for her. Gradually she began inching her way back into our yard, acting as though it were her own.

At first she came into our yard and pulled up part of the ivy. When I asked her why, she said she'd planted it in the first place and she could do it if she wanted to. Then she began trimming trees limbs, starting with the ones she could reach and then sneaking in a ladder when we weren't at home. Finally, after years of pleading, we did what we should have done in the first place. We put up a fence.

This reminds me of what Satan tries to do in our lives. Before we knew Jesus Christ, Satan pretended we were his. He planted thoughts in our minds, sinful acts in our wills, and insecurities in our emotions. But God purchased us at a very high price and we became His treasured possession.

Satan knows where the boundary line around our heart lies, but just like Mrs. Smith, he attempts to creep back in to plant a little thought here, a little temptation there, and the next thing you know he's standing on a ladder trimming our trees! Well, maybe not our trees, but he's lopping off areas of growth and whacking at anything within his reach.

So what do you do when you see the enemy creeping back onto your purchased territory? You show him the title deed signed by God and put up a fence of faith to keep him out. Works every time.

Take a good look at your life today. Do you see any boundary lines that have grown fuzzy? Are there any areas where you've let Satan make himself at home? Maybe it's time to get out the title deed and tell him to get off God's property.

Dear Lord, how thankful I am that You own the title deed to my heart. I praise Your name that I never have to worry about the devil taking possession of it again. In Jesus' name, amen.

ADDITIONAL SCRIPTURE READING: PSALM 16:1-8

65

Weed Control

*Reckless words pierce like a sword, but the
tongue of the wise brings healing.*

PROVERBS 12:18

After Steve and I built our first home, we hauled in truckloads of rich topsoil and spread it over our rocky ground. Then we planted thousands of tiny fescue grass seeds. After several weeks of watering, slender blades of green began to push their way through the dirt in search of sunlight. Within six weeks, our yard was a carpet of luscious grass that beckoned us to kick off our shoes and walk barefoot across the lawn.

The following spring, I noticed a few unwelcome visitors in my prized lawn: dandelions, crabgrass, and ground ivy.

"Steve," I asked, "where did these weeds come from?"

"They came from seeds that blew in from other places," he replied. "Mostly they came from our neighbors' yards."

After the grass came up, all the green blended together nicely, and we hardly noticed the weeds. However, the next spring we had more weeds and less grass. By the fourth spring, we knew that if we didn't apply some sort of weed control, soon we would have a yard full of weeds and no grass at all.

Then God reminded me that my yard was a picture of the words we speak in marriage. During the dating and courting days, we tend to shower our prospective mate with seeds of encouraging words, compliments, adoration, and praise. After we are married, the weeds begin to creep in and sprout up: a sarcastic comment here, a critical jab there, and a nagging spirit in between. As time passes, if we do not give attention to the weed problem, we are in danger of having a yard full of weeds with no grass at all—a marriage full of criticism with not an encouraging word to be heard.

How do we stop the weeds from spreading? Prayer, the power of the Holy Spirit, and a heart determined to keep our marriage weed-free. Eliminating verbal weeds doesn't happen overnight, especially if the weeds have taken root and already had their damaging effects. But with consistent, persistent determination, we can eliminate the life-choking weeds and once again sport a beautiful marriage that is the envy of all the homes in the neighborhood.

> *Every plant has little seeds*
> *That make others of its kind.*
> *Apple seeds make apple tress*
> *And they'll do it every time.*
>
> *Seeds make flowers, shrubs, and trees,*
> *Seeds make ferns, vines, and weeds.*
> *What you plant is what you grow.*
> *So be careful what you sow.*
>
> AUTHOR UNKNOWN

As you are listening to God today, listen to yourself as well. Are your words weeds that choke the life out of others, or are they seeds that take root and lift others up?

Dear Lord, help me weed out words that are choking the life from my relationships. I pray I will sow good words into the hearts and souls of all I come in contact with today. In Jesus' name, amen.

ADDITIONAL SCRIPTURE READING: JAMES 3:1-12

66

The Learner's Permit

Instruct the wise and they will be wiser still;
teach the righteous and they will add to their learning.

PROVERBS 9:9 TNIV

I had dreaded the day for months. My lunch stuck in my throat, not making it past the lump lodged there. I knew the momentous day was coming. I had fifteen and a half years to prepare, but that had proved insufficient. Would I live through the ordeal? Could I withstand the pressure? Should I allow the inevitable?

"Hi, Mom!" Steven chirped as he eagerly burst through the kitchen door to disrupt my musings. "I'm home from school. Ready to go get my driver's permit?"

"Hi, son. I'd almost forgotten about it," I teased. "Was that today?"

"Mom, you *know* it's today. It's been marked on the calendar for weeks, and you even made the appointment at the DMV so we wouldn't have to wait!"

What was I thinking?

"Oh, yeah," I said. "I remember. Let me gather my things."

I puttered around the house, stalling for time. "Purse, keys, Steven's Social Security card, insurance information, Tylenol, nerve medication—okay. I'm ready to go."

I knew Steven was prepared. He had studied three times more for his driver's permit exam than he had for his biology semester exam. After all, which was more important? He was ready. I wasn't.

We arrived at the ever-crowded DMV, where we filled out the necessary papers. I paced the waiting room with several other apprehensive parents while Steven took the test. Of course he passed. Of course he wanted to drive home—on a Friday afternoon, in five o'clock traffic, on a major highway. It was the longest 12 miles of my life.

As we neared a busy intersection close to our home, I saw the traffic light turning yellow. Did he see it? I wasn't sure.

"Steven," I managed to say through clenched teeth as we rapidly approached. "Are you going to stop?"

"I don't know. Should I stop or try to get through?"

In his indecision he came to a screeching halt—right smack-dab in the middle of the intersection where we sat idling over a manhole. Cars on the east, west, north, and south, stared in disbelief.

"Now what?" he yelped in a voice an octave higher than normal.

"Back up."

"What?" he asked.

"Back up."

The car behind us graciously backed up and let Steven shimmy into position behind the red light, which promptly turned green. Whew! That was close.

Later that afternoon he ran a stop sign in a parking lot, declaring he never knew parking lots even had traffic signs.

After our eventful day, I decided Steven did not have a *driver's* permit. He had a *learner's* permit. He had permission *to learn*—and learn he would.

I wonder if perhaps I got a taste of how our heavenly Father feels as His children embark on their Christian journey. Like Steven passing the written test, we might think we know all the rules, can keep life under control, know when to stop, go, slow down, and speed up. Then we see a yellow light from the Lord and wonder—*Does that mean to slow down or speed up?*

I don't know about you, but I've been caught in the intersection of life more times than I'd like to admit. I've had times when I couldn't decide whether to go forward or back up. As a result, I found myself idling in the middle, holding up traffic.

On those days I think God is saying, *Back up. That's right. Back up and wait until I give you a green light.* I've decided that when it comes to driving down the road of life, I only have my learner's permit. He has never given me permission to take hold of the wheel and apply my foot to the accelerator without Him in the car.

How about you? Who's hold the steering wheel of your life today?

⌒

Dear Heavenly Father, forgive me when I try to take control of my life. Forgive me when I act as though I know it all. I don't. I am still learning. Thank You for being the patient Teacher and showing me when to stop, yield, or go. In Jesus' name, amen.

ADDITIONAL SCRIPTURE READING:
PSALM 119:9-16,33-40,97-99,105

67

Then God Said, "It Is Good"

God saw all that he had made, and it was very good.

GENESIS 1:31

It's 7:05 a.m. I'm sitting on my patio with a cup of steaming coffee in my hand and my Bible in my lap. Quietly, God whispers, *Listen.*

"What, Lord?" I answer. "Are You going to tell me something special?"

Just listen.

I close my eyes and let my ears paint a picture on the canvas of my mind.

A robin sweetly sings. She's answered by a crow's caw. A red bird chirps, and a high-pitched staccato tweet interrupts. A dove coos sweet nothings to his lifetime mate, and she returns coos in reply. An orchestra of at least 12 different birds fills the air, like instruments tuning before act 1, scene 1, of the day.

The telephone rings and I am startled back to reality as the taskmaster beckons with its litany of demands and requests. The day has begun, and I promise to sit with the Lord once again at day's end.

It's 7:05 p.m. I am sitting on my patio with a steaming cup of coffee in my hand and a much-loved book in my lap. Once again, God says, *Listen.*

"Are You going to tell me something special?"

Just listen.

The birds are still singing but their songs are masked by other noises filling the air. Cars roar as they speed down the nearby highway. A plane soars overhead, leaving a trail of rumble following behind. A violin whines as a child practices her lessons. A little girl squeals with delight as she is being chased by her daddy just home from work. A rhythmic thump echoes on the concrete as a teenage boy bounces a basketball on the sidewalk. An ambulance siren pierces the evening as it heads to rescue someone in distress.

The phone rings again, but this time I do not answer. The Lord calls me to sit still and think about the two bookends of my day.

I thought about the beauty of the undisturbed morning with nature awakening to a new day. That must have been a taste of what God heard on the day of creation before He created man, but He chose to fashion us regardless. He knew what we would do, the cacophony of sounds we would introduce into His perfect world, the laughing, crying, sirens, cars, airplanes, trucks—all drowning out the sound of His creation. And yet He chose to create us anyway. Amazingly, knowing what He knew, He looked at us and said, "It is good."

God was letting me know that no matter how much noise we make, no matter how much mess we make, if He had it all to do over again, He wouldn't change a thing.

Shhh. Be still. Listen. What do you hear?

⌒

Dear Lord, sometimes I wonder why You bother with us at all. And yet You love us. You looked at man and woman in the Garden of Eden and said, "It is good." I am amazed at Your great love for me. I love You so much. In Jesus' name, amen.

ADDITIONAL SCRIPTURE READING: GENESIS 1:1–2:3

68

Who's Talking?

This is my Son, whom I love. Listen to him!

MARK 9:7

Fourteen exhausted and sweaty teenage boys plopped down on the bottom step of the gymnasium bleachers. The assistant junior varsity basketball coach paced back and forth, lecturing them on the error of their ways. In the style of Sergeant Carter addressing Gomer Pyle, he yelled, "Who's talking?"

The boys, in practiced unison, shouted back, "You are, sir!"

"Okay, then. Listen up!" he barked.

For the next 15 minutes, they did just that.

Unfortunately for this merry band of athletes, school was not simply a place where sports were played but also an institution for academic advancement. It was time to see just how much advancement had taken place in the first four months of school via the dreaded semester exams.

Six of the basketball players sat nervously with their peers on the edge of their seats. Each grasped pencils in hand, ready to attack the 20-page social studies test. Apparently, someone broke the total silence code with a whisper. The 6' 5", 250-pound teacher jumped to attention and yelled, "Who's talking?"

Without even thinking, Chris Crutchfield, one of the basketball teammates, shot back, "You are, sir!"

The high school freshman social studies class erupted with peals of laughter. Everyone was tickled, except the teacher and the terrified Chris.

"So, you want to be smart, do you?" Mr. Thompson asked. "Who else in here wants to be smart?"

More than half of the class (mostly boys overcome with mischief, my son included) raised their hands. "I want to be smart," they answered back.

Things were not going well for Mr. Thompson or for Chris Crutch-field. After-school detention was crowded the next day.

It was an innocent mistake. An automatic response. A reflex reaction. But it made Chris a hero for the day among his buddies. And, in a way, he was my hero as well.

When my heavenly Teacher speaks to me with that still, small voice, I want to recognize Him. When He asks, "Who's talking?" I pray my response will be just as automatic as Chris's. "You are, Sir!" And when He says, "Well, then. Listen up," that's exactly what I plan to do.

The more time we spend listening to God through His Word, prayer, the Holy Spirit, creation, and circumstances, the clearer His voice becomes.

~

Heavenly Father, help me be quick to hear Your voice and quick to respond. Speak, Lord. I'm listening. In Jesus' name, amen.

ADDITIONAL SCRIPTURE READING: JOHN 10:1-18

69

The Guest Book

You yourselves are our letter, written on our hearts,
known and read by everybody.

2 Corinthians 3:2

Just before leaving our rented condominium after a week of sun, sand, and surf at Hilton Head Island, we found a treasure tucked under some old magazines on the coffee table. It was a guest book signed by previous vacationers who had also shared a relaxing week away from home.

Feeling somewhat like a peeping Tom craning to peer into someone's window, we cracked open the book and stole a glimpse into the personalities of our fellow travelers. With each entry we visualized what the guests looked like, decided if we would like to invite them over for dinner, and surmised whether they had an enjoyable vacation together.

Have a look for yourself and decide with whom you would like to share a cup of coffee or would like to have as your neighbor:

- Thank you very much for the use of your condo. We thoroughly enjoyed our first but not last visit to South Carolina.

- Had a great time. Enjoyed your villa very much! However, you need to have the springs in the couch repaired. Very uncomfortable to sit on. Thank you.

- We have decided this is where we'd love to live. It's a golfer's dream. Your courses are beautiful. The girls loved the beach, parasailing, bike rides, horseback riding, shopping! I love my tan. We will be back to visit! If you are ever in Arkansas, come to Stuttgart. We are 50 miles east of Little Rock. Stuttgart hosts the World Championship Duck Calling Contest every year during Thanksgiving weekend.

We are known as the "Rice and Duck Capital of the World." Riceland Rice comes from our little town, and the ducks feed off of the rice fields during the winter after harvest. It is some of the best duck hunting anywhere. Thank you for the use of your condo. We've had a great week here. P. S. Bill and Hillary said to tell you "Hi, y'all!"

- We really enjoyed your villa, but we won't be staying here again. We just booked another villa at Colonnade for next year a couple of doors down for almost $300 less.

- Hello. My name is Amanda and I got here yesterday. So far we are having a good time. I'm eleven years old and I came here with my mother, grandmother, and my Aunt Loretta. She got here at the same time we did, but she is leaving tomorrow. We came all the way from Lake Wylie, South Carolina. I love it here and might be back next year.

- It has been a fabulous time. This villa is bigger than our home! My niece is sure she saw a whale at the Old Oyster Factory, but we are sure she saw a buoy. Greg and Dad played golf together and we all played mini golf. We went bike riding and "gator chasing." The ocean is breathtaking. I've never seen it before, so I'm still in awe! I love the wildlife, and my turtle friend says, "Hi!"

- When we first came, the keys wouldn't fit, you forgot to give us a pass, and we almost ran over a biker. Get better service! Two grandmas were with us! Sixth time here— never happened before.

Pretty revealing, wouldn't you say? As we rated each guest from one to ten, I thought about the entries I have written with my daily life. First Chronicles 29:15 calls us "aliens" in the NIV and "sojourners and tenants" in the NASB. We are guests on this earth. Our real home is in heaven.

What entries am I writing with my attitudes, actions, and words for the entire world to see? Will they think I was a crabby old lady who wanted better service? Will they think I savored each day here with my wonderful family? Will they think I would have preferred another life just a few doors down? Or will they think I so enjoyed my time here that I wanted to share it with anyone and everyone who was passing through?

What are you writing on the guest book pages of your life today?

⌒

Heavenly Father, I love You with all my heart,
and I don't want it to be a secret. Help me to live a life
so that others will know it. In Jesus' name, amen.

ADDITIONAL SCRIPTURE READING: 2 CORINTHIANS 3:1-6

Circles in the Sand

The Lord your God has given you the land.
Go up and take possession of it as the Lord,
the God of your fathers, told you.
Do not be afraid; do not be discouraged.

DEUTERONOMY 1:21

I was sitting on my sofa doing some paperwork when I noticed a large red fire ant crawling across my sand-colored carpet. Being that I was comfortably molded into the seat cushion, I didn't want to get up. So I waited until the ant was within striking distance before I reached for my shoe to put an abrupt end to his journey. The carpet was just a few months old and I didn't want Mr. Ant's remains to leave a permanent mark, so I just banged on him softly. Just in case he wasn't "all the way dead," I left my shoe lying on top of him until I was ready to get up.

To my surprise, a few minutes later, a shaken ant eased his way out from underneath his leather prison and began to limp away. I guess his vision, equilibrium, or left side was impaired, because instead of making a mad dash toward the door, he began to totter, making a series of left turns and going in circles.

Thirty minutes later Steve walked into the room. "There's a big ant crawling on the floor."

"Yeah, I know," I nonchalantly replied.

"Why don't you get a tissue and get rid of him?" he asked.

"I will when I get up."

"Aren't you afraid he'll crawl away by that time?"

"Nope," I responded confidently. "He's been going around in circles for 30 minutes. He's not going anywhere."

But then he started walking straight toward the door, so I got up and took care of it.

This scenario made me think about another creature who traveled in circles. Well, a lot of creatures, in fact. About two million Israelites—and not for 40 minutes, but for 40 years.

The Israelites had been under the Egyptians' shoe for 400 years. Then God called Moses to convince Pharaoh that their brick-making days were over and it was time for them to move on. Moses was to lead this band of slaves to freedom—to a land flowing with milk and honey. With plagues that would excite any professional exterminator, God convinced Pharaoh that letting the Israelites go would be a good idea. Pharaoh yelled, "Get those Israelites out of here!"

So they gathered up their belongings (not to mention a few belongings that weren't theirs) and left. Led by a pillar of fire by night and a cloud by day, they moved forward. After marching between the towering walls of the parted waters of the Red Sea, they sang for joy. "Hip, hip, hooray. Now we're on our way." Or so it seemed.

But they didn't joyously parade on to the land flowing with milk and honey. They didn't continue in reverence and awe of a God who had already performed more miracles in their presence than most people see in a thousand lifetimes. Instead, they started to grumble and complain: "We're sick of this food." They started to doubt God: "Did He bring us out here to die?" They started to question Moses' leadership: "What are we going to drink?" They bickered among themselves, argued with Moses, and disobeyed God. And each time they stiffened their necks, God told them to take a left turn.

For 40 years they wandered in circles in the sand until an entire generation died out and a new generation was born. One day the stiff necks' prodigy had an "aha" moment. "Hey," they reasoned, "let's try obeying God and see where that leads us."

Of course, we know where it led them. It led them to where obedience to God always leads—on a straight path to the Promised Land.

As I studied the Israelites' journey, I noticed a strange phenomenon. As long as they were going in circles in the desert and bickering among themselves, they didn't encounter many outside enemies. They didn't fight many battles. There was only one.

But as soon as they crossed over the Jordan and headed in the path called obedience, they were under attack left and right. And so it is with us today. Many have been led out of Egypt (saved from the bondage of sin) and passed through the Red Sea (Jesus' blood) only to continue their Christian walk going in circles. And, amazingly, in the circular walk, there are very few battles. It's safe—not much action. Satan doesn't need to spend his energy attacking a bunch of desert circlers because they are no threat to him. But let a freed child of God start walking in obedience and moving toward the Promised Land of Christian maturity, and the battle's on.

Are you experiencing spiritual warfare in your life? Are you encountering Jebusites, Amalekites, Hittites, Gossip-ites, Mocker-ites, In-law-ites, and Neighbor-ites? Well, praise the Lord! It must mean you're headed in the right direction.

Dear God, hallelujah! I have battles left and right! That must mean Satan sees me as a threat. Give me the courage to keep moving forward in obedience, knowing that my personal Promised Land of the abundant life comes from listening to You and walking in the direction You lead. In Jesus' name, amen.

ADDITIONAL SCRIPTURE READING: JOSHUA 1:1-18

71

I Have Called You by Name

*Fear not, for I have redeemed you; I have
called you by name, you are mine.*

ISAIAH 43:1 ESV

"Daddy," I whispered. "Don't you know who I am?"

There have been several people in my life who never seem to remember my name. Some of my more popular aliases are Sarah James, Susan James, Shannon James, and Jane Jaynes. Then there are the people who just can't remember me altogether and don't try to fish a name from their memory pool. To tell you the truth, it has never really bothered me. After all, I'm not very good with names either.

But names are very important to God. In the Bible, a person's name often revealed a unique quality of their character. "Moses" meant "drawn out of water." "Ruth" meant "woman friend." "Naomi" meant "pleasant," and she later changed her name to "Mara," which meant "bitter." Her two sons' names, "Mahlon" and "Kilion," meant "Puny" and "Piney." Needless to say, these two fellows weren't exactly strapping young broncos, and they died at an early age. If a person had an encounter with the living God, many times He changed their name. "Abram" was changed to "Abraham." "Sarai" was changed to "Sarah." And "Saul" was changed to "Paul."

Yes, names are very important. That's why when someone very dear to me forgot mine, it broke my heart.

A few years after I was married, I noticed my dad becoming very forgetful. At first it was small things: forgetting an order at work, misplacing his shoes or keys, not remembering what day it was, drawing a blank on a close friend's name. Then it progressed to more serious absentminded behavior: forgetting where he parked in a parking deck; coming home to take my mom to the market, forgetting he had taken her already an hour before; and becoming confused when taking measurements for cabinets, a task he had been doing for some 30 years. Finally our greatest fears were confirmed. Dad had Alzheimer's disease. He was 56 years old.

My dad had been a tough cookie as a young man. He ran a building supply business and was well respected in the business community of our small town. From the time he was 56 to 66, I watched a strapping, quick-witted entrepreneur reduced to a man who could not remember how to speak, button his shirt, or move a spoon from his plate to his mouth. But my most heart-wrenching day was the day he forgot my name.

I still remember holding his face in my hands and saying, "Daddy, it's me. Do you know who I am?" But I was only met by a childish grin and eyes that seemed to look straight through me.

In Isaiah 49:1, the prophet announces, "Before I was born the LORD called me; from my birth he has made mention of my name."

God knows your name, and the Bible promises He will never forget it. And if we listen closely, perhaps in the vibrant hues of a sunset, the gentle breeze off the ocean, or the soft patter of falling snow, we'll hear Him gently calling. *Fear not, for I have redeemed you; I have called you by name, you are mine.*

~

*Heavenly Father, thank You for calling me by name
and inscribing it on the palm of Your hand. I know
You will never forget me or forget about me, but I'll
always be on Your mind. In Jesus' name, amen.*

ADDITIONAL SCRIPTURE READING: ISAIAH 43:1-19

72

Keeping Going! You Can Do It!

*Since we are surrounded by such a great cloud of
witnesses, let us throw off everything that hinders
and the sin that so easily entangles, and let us run
with perseverance the race marked out for us.*

It's a bird! It's a plane! No, it's Steven's shoe!"

My son was fast, and he ran with a fast crowd. As a matter of fact, his entire track team was pretty fast. In the ninth grade, Steven participated in the conference track meet, running the 1600 meters. (That's four times around the big circle.) I was so proud of him as he ran like a gazelle around the first lap, about six feet behind the first-place participant. But, at some point during the beginning of the second lap, we saw an unidentified flying object soar over Steven's head.

"What was that?" my husband asked.

"It's Steven's shoe!" I exclaimed.

All the fans were laughing and pointing as we noticed that Steven's left running shoe had come untied, flown heavenward, and landed on the grassy field. But the amazing thing was that Steven never missed a beat. With the right shoe still intact, he ran on. All curious eyes were now on one runner. Would he stop? Would he slow down? Would his sock stay on?

His teammates began to run around the track, cheering him on. "Go Steven! Don't slow down!"

Surprisingly, he sped up. By the third lap, he had passed the first-place runner by several paces. But then, predictably, his sock started to work its way down his ankle and the toe was flopping like a loose sole of a worn old shoe. Undaunted, Steven ran on, his sock flopping all the while. The race became a contest not to see who would come in first, but to see if Steven's sock would make it to the end.

When he crossed the finish line in first place, the crowd erupted in applause and laughter. He had recorded a personal best!

"Son, maybe you should have kicked off both shoes. No tellin' what you could have done. You made your best time ever. What made the difference?" we asked.

Steven answered, "I knew everybody was looking at me. It wasn't just a race anymore. They were watching to see what I'd do. It made me go faster. It made me want to do better."

Then God began to speak to my heart about what I had just seen. I can run this race called "life" right along with the rest of the crowd and no one may notice at all. But when adversity strikes, that's when all eyes turn to one small runner. "Will she buckle? Will she quit? Will she turn back?" spectators ask.

But when we press on, despite the struggle of life, despite the laughter of the crowd, we'll hear the applause of heaven and the encouraging cheers of our heavenly Father cheering us on. And onlookers will be amazed at the courageous persistence only God can give.

Dear Lord, as I go through the struggles of life, help me to press on with courage and confidence so that those watching will see the peace that only comes from knowing You. In Jesus' name, amen.

ADDITIONAL SCRIPTURE READING: HEBREWS 12:1-13

73

Playing with the Pros

We all, like sheep, have gone astray.

ISAIAH 53:6

Golf. I just don't understand the draw. Men and women spend millions of dollars on the sport, and for what? Frustration, consternation, evaluation, exaggeration…and all for supposed relaxation.

One vacation we rented a condominium which overlooked the eighth fairway of a golf course. Steven and I got up early one morning and sat out on the deck. It was a tranquil setting. A weeping willow draping into a meandering canal served as a boundary between our backyard and the fairway. A loon craned his long neck to sip from the stream. Turtles basked in the sun, and birds sang to welcome in a new day. One thing I can say about golf, the scenery is definitely enticing.

The tee box for the eighth hole was in view, so we decided to watch and see how the pros played the game. The fairway was lined on the right by beautiful homes and on the left by the canal that ran in front of our porch. These guys had probably been playing golf all their lives—at least their outfits and clubs made it appear that way. They were decked out in the latest Links Fashion: polo knit shirts with designer logos, pleated khaki pants, snazzy wing tip spiked shoes, and occasionally a matching cap. Oh, yes. They were looking good.

"They have to be good," Steven said. "It costs sixty-five dollars to play this course. Who would pay that much money if you didn't know what you were doing?"

Who indeed? I thought to myself.

Ping went the familiar sound of a metal club coming in contact with the dimpled white ball. *Splash* went the sound of the hooked ball as it landed in the water.

Ping! Another sound as a club made contact. *Bonk!* The thud of a sliced ball as it bounced off a rooftop.

This was more entertaining than we had imagined. We had to hold our hands over our mouths to keep the disgruntled bag shaggers from hearing our laughter. Of the 40 "expert" golfers we watched tee off that morning, eight sliced their balls into the backyards of the aligning homes and ten hooked theirs into the canal. Balls bounced off roofs, hid in tall grasses, ricocheted off trees, and trespassed into flower gardens. Occasionally, and I mean occasionally, a golfer hit a ball straight and long with perfect form and trajectory.

"Steven," I said, "what you are seeing today is life being played out before your very eyes. As we play the game of life, some people look good, have the right clothes, buy the best toys, and even know the right lingo. But that doesn't make them a pro. We all slice, hook, and get off course at times. It's the rare person who drives it straight down the middle and stays on the fairway throughout the entire course. The only players who do tend to stay on course more often than not are the ones who practice regularly. But it's not only practice that makes you successful. Many golfers go to classes but refuse to change their old harmful habits. Therefore, they continue to repeat the same mistakes time and time again. It's hard to change a bad swing or a bad habit once it is established, but it can be done."

"What I don't get," he said, "is why these guys keep on playing. They look so frustrated!"

"I think it's because occasionally they hit a good shot and it gives them hope," I answered. "They hope that one day they will be able to drive more balls straight down the middle than to the left or right, and that dream keeps them trying."

God used that moment to speak to both Steven and me. Oh, that we would have the same driving determination as a golfer. The chance of ever getting a hole in one is very unlikely, but that doesn't keep him or her from trying.

About the time Steven and I finished watching the golfers, my husband walked in and tossed his clubs on the floor.

"How'd you play today?" I asked.

"Don't ask," he replied. "But I did hit a couple of good shots."

Steven and I just looked at each other and laughed.

Dear Lord, thank You for the small victories in life that encourage me to keep on keeping on. As I continue facing daily challenges, I will continue depending on You and standing on Your promises. In Jesus' name, amen.

ADDITIONAL SCRIPTURE READING: MATTHEW 7:24-27

74

Just a Bit Off-Key

Make a joyful noise to the LORD, all the earth!

PSALM 100:1 ESV

I love to hear the familiar sound of church bells ringing the hour in the distance. There's something about it that reminds me that God is near and time is in His hands. Occasionally, the bells near our home play a familiar hymn for the entire community to enjoy. Well, at least that's the plan. But the truth is, the bells are just a bit off-key, and if the sound wasn't coming from a church steeple, the neighbors would probably call in a noise complaint.

One day, as I winced at the church bells' rendition of "Amazing Grace," God reminded me of His. Many of us folks who fill churches each week are...well, a little bit off-key too.

I've always felt sorry for pastors. These men and women have every word from their mouths scrutinized, analyzed, and criticized. When I was growing up, my pastor had a tendency to combine two words and create a new one. For example: beautiful and gorgeous might be combined to be "beautimous." Or elation and a loud auditory expression might be combined to form "elationatory."

When Steve and I were making our wedding plans, we decided we would write our own wedding vows so no new vocabulary words would be invented at our expense. We wrote and repeated our own vows, but invited the pastor to say his own closing prayer.

"Oh, Lord," he began, "Thou hast brought into creality..."

I'm not sure what else he said. Steve and I peeped up at each other and mouthed, "Creality?" Then our shoulders started shaking, trying to hold back the giggles. I'm sure the congregation, seeing our shaking shoulders, thought we were overcome with emotion and trying to hold back our tears.

I remember another church faux pas when my friend Karen and I went to hear an acquaintance of hers preach his very first sermon. It was in a very formal "First Something or Nother" church with tall white columns and mountainous brick steps leading up to heavy white double doors. The young intern approached the pulpit, dressed in his black robe and looking very holy indeed. Then he boomed in his best preacher voice. "Let us pray." (Long pause) "Almiiiiighty Gog."

Yes, he said "Gog." The word just hung in the air for several moments.

Then there was my friend Ellen's wedding. She was married in a little white church in the wildwood of eastern North Carolina. For sentimental reasons, the family invited an elderly retired pastor to officiate part of the ceremony. I guess he could not hear very well, and he apparently thought neither could we. During the repeating of the vows, he yelled, "Do you, Ellen, take this man to be your lawfully wedded husband in sickness and in death?"

Ellen just stood there. I could almost hear her thoughts saying, "You mean in sickness and health, don't you?" I'm not sure what she ended up saying because our entire row of college mates got a bad case of the giggles, and we were more concerned with not disrupting the ceremony than hearing her answer. But as far as I know, Ellen and her hubby are doing fine, in sickness and in health.

Of course it's not just leaders who blunder. We're all a bunch of mere humans who need God's amazing grace.

Come to think about it, the off-key church bells seem very appropriate. God puts the song in our hearts, and while we sing with all our might, sometimes it comes out just a bit off-key. Perhaps that's why the psalmist wrote, "Make a joyful noise unto the LORD, all ye lands" (Psalm 100:1 KJV). He knew that even our feeble attempts at praise, blunders and all, are still music to God's ears.

Today, try singing a song from your heart. Don't worry if it is off-key. God doesn't mind at all. After all, He's used to it.

And when you see someone who's a bit off-key as well, just smile and hum a bar of "Amazing Grace."

Dear Lord, sometimes the song of my life is not very melodious, but I will still sing praises to Your name and make a joyful noise. I know it is music to Your ears. In Jesus' name, amen.

ADDITIONAL SCRIPTURE READING: PSALM 100:1-5

75

Fogged In

*"I know the plans I have for you," declares the
Lord, "plans to prosper you and not to harm
you, plans to give you hope and a future."*

JEREMIAH 29:11

The night before I left for a trip from Charlotte to Kentucky, via a plane change in Atlanta, I made careful preparations. The conference had been booked a year ago, and I was eager to be with the women who would be gathering in just a few hours. But the next morning proved to be the beginning of one of those days that the harder I tried, the behinder I got. It all began at 6:35 a.m.

We left home with plenty of time, but an unexpected wall of fog reduced our drive to the airport to a congested crawl. I made it to the airport just as the plane was supposed to be boarding. At 8:59, I bolted from the car, through the terminal doors, and to the security checkpoint. Faster than Superman in a phone booth, I stripped off my boots, jacket, earrings, necklace, and watch, pushed my carry-on through the X-ray monster's mouth, and walked through the metal arches. "Ma'am, we're going to have to check inside your luggage. There's something in there we can't identify."

"No, please don't," I pled. "I'm about to miss my plane."

"No, please don't," doesn't go over too well with security guards. So they did—search my bag that is. Inside they discovered 25 Scripture bracelets that read, "I can do all things through Christ who gives me strength." I almost laughed.

While they searched, I redressed and reaccessorized. *Please, Lord, let the flight be delayed,* I prayed. I jogged to the gate in my three-inch heel boots only to discover that God had answered my prayers! The flight was delayed. It seemed I wasn't the only one affected by the fog. Over the next 45 minutes, I summoned my sanity and slowed my pulse.

Finally, we were on the plane and on our way. But then…rolling, rolling, rolling, pause. Rolling, rolling, rolling, pause. It seemed that we were going to drive to Atlanta rather than fly. We sat on the runway for 45 more minutes, and I knew I was not going to make my connecting flight.

When we did finally arrive, two and a half hours behind schedule, I discovered that my flight to Kentucky was canceled and there were no more seats available for the entire day. I was placed on standby, only to join 40 others on standby as well. I was number 32. The plane held 57 passengers and was booked solid. I called the conference coordinator and gave her the news. Prognosis—not good. My attitude—even worse.

Now, I have left out lots of frustrating, minute details, but let's just say I was not happy. No one was cooperating: the weather, the airlines, nor the One who controls it all. At least that's how I felt. Pull up a chair beside me and watch what God did to adjust my attitude and put the day's frustrations in perspective.

I'm sitting at a jam-packed gate filled with angry and disgruntled passengers. I look just like them, feel just like them, act just like them. You with me?

"Excuse me," the airport employee announced. "Let's clear the aisle, people. This plane is preparing to disembark. Clear the way. Make room."

She walked over to the boarding door and positioned a red wheelchair by the entrance. Then she was joined by another, then another, then another. I had a front row seat and facing me—staring me in the face—were seven attendees standing behind seven shiny red wheelchairs, waiting for passengers disembarking the plane.

Then God began to speak to my heart. I suspect He had been trying to get my attention all day long, but I was too wrapped up in my own struggles to listen. *Sharon*, He began, *which side of this aisle would you rather be on. The standby side, or the side waiting for those who can't stand at all?*

Suddenly my little trials and tribulations of the day seemed very small. So what if my flight was canceled? I could walk. I stopped whining and began thanking God—for eyes that see, ears that hear, fingers that feel, hands that help, lips that speak. I realized I needed to focus less on the air traffic controllers and more on the One who controls the air. A little fog never stopped Him from accomplishing all that He has purposed, and if He wanted me to sit in that airport, I could trust that He had a great plan.

I didn't make that flight, but all of us on standby did get out of Atlanta that night. A family of five made it to the wedding of a beloved son, a soldier in uniform returned to the arms of his waiting mom, and I made it to the conference with 30 minutes to spare.

God had it under control all along. He just needed to lift the fog in my own heart before I could see clearly to serve Him.

Today, let's choose to thank God for His provision and protection, even if foggy circumstances sometimes block our view.

⌐

Dear Heavenly Father, there are many days when I become so anxious about the details of life. Thank you for the reminder that You are in control. Direct my path. Help me rest in the assurance that no matter what happens today, it is no surprise to You. In Jesus' name, amen.

⌐

ADDITIONAL SCRIPTURE READING: ISAIAH 55:1-13

76

A Not So Quiet Quiet Time

He put a new song in my mouth, a hymn of praise to our God.

PSALM 40:3

"Could you please be quiet and leave me alone?" I commanded the squawking bird. "You are completely ruining my quiet time with God!"

My flower gardens were at their peak, bursting with fuchsia, red and white impatiens, begonias, and blue ageratum. The hanging baskets next to my patio chair were heavy with purple and pink velvety petunias, filling the air with a sweet fragrance not found in the finest department stores. It was one of those perfect peaceful storybook mornings.

I sat down close enough to the baskets to keep the scent of the petunias wafting past my nose. Suddenly, a little finch darted from the flower basket that had become his summer home. He perched on a tree in front of me, angrily squawking in my direction. His bride came and perched beside him and sang a lovely song, but there was no chance of calming her man. He hopped around from the tree to the chair to the wall to the table. Pointing his beak in my direction, he demanded that I move. So much for a quiet time.

Finally, after 45 minutes of this constant badgering, I could take it no longer and decided to give this bird a piece of my mind. "Look, buddy," I said, "who planted those flower baskets in the first place? I did! Who hung and fertilized them? I did! And who waters them daily? I do! Don't you come out here complaining to me because I chose to sit here and enjoy what I've planted. They're mine in the first place—not yours. I'm just letting you live there. And you should be thankful for that. Besides, you're making a terrible mess!"

He continued hurling insults my way, and after a while I realized his angry complaints had a familiar ring to them. In fact, they sounded a lot like my own. Oh, how I complain when situations don't go my way, when someone messes up my plans, or when someone invades my space. My, my, my.

I opened the pages of my Bible to Psalm 24:1: "The earth is the LORD's, and everything in it." Then God began to speak to my heart. *Who made this earth in the first place? Who planted and watered all you have before you? This whole earth and all it contains is Mine. I'm just letting you live here. And sometimes you make a terrible mess. Stop your squawking and start chirping the song I've put in your heart.*

It was not a very quiet quiet time, but God's message came through loud and clear.

What's God saying to your heart today? Are you squawking about with ruffled feathers or chirping a thankful song?

⌇

Dear Lord, thank You for noisy quiet times when You speak to my heart loud and clear. Please speak to me today. I'm listening. In Jesus' name, amen.

ADDITIONAL SCRIPTURE READING: PSALM 40:1-17

77

Go, Stu!

Encourage one another.

1 THESSALONIANS 5:11

The boys lined up on the starting mark. The starter's pistol fired, and 70 cross-country runners left in a cloud of dust and cheers. My nephew, Stu, was among the herd.

I don't know if you have ever been to a cross-country race, but it is not exactly a spectator sport. Runners line up on the starting mark, a gun fires to begin, and then the participants disappear down a trail in the woods only to reappear 16 minutes later.

When I attended one of Stu's cross country races, his friends assured me that the most exciting part of the race was not the runners running, but Stu's mother, Pat, cheering. As soon as Stu's foot left the starting line, Pat picked up her megaphone and moved into action. "GO, STU!" she yelled.

The boys disappeared down the 3.2-mile trail in the woods, but that didn't deter Pat's enthusiasm. "Go, Stu!" she continued to yell as she ran to strategic spots along the trail where the boys would pass by. My embarrassed husband stood a safe distance away, pretending he didn't know who we were. Pat had no shame.

"Pat, do you think he can hear you when he's deep in the woods?" I asked.

"I don't know, but if there's a chance he can, I want him to hear my voice cheering for him."

At one point she yelled, "GO, STU!" and a man echoed back, "He can't heeeaaar yooouuu." That didn't deter her. For 16 minutes this dynamo continued to pump confidence and courage into her son's heart.

After the race I approached my nephew. "Stu, when you're running in the woods, can you hear your mother cheering for you?"

"Oh, yes," he said, "I can hear her the whole way."

"And what does that do for you?"

"It makes me not want to quit. When my legs and lungs ache, or when I feel like I'm going to get sick, I hear my mom cheering for me, and it makes me not want to stop."

What a beautiful picture of the encouragement we can give each other in the great race of life. An encouraging word, offered at just the right moment, could mean the difference between someone finishing well or collapsing along the way. Can't you just hear it now? "Go, Susan! You can do it!" "Keep it up, Mary! You're going to make it!" "Don't quit, Janet! I'm right behind you!" We can make a difference in the lives of our friends and families by being that encouraging voice in the distance, that perpetual cheerleader on the front lines, or that pep band of praise in the echo of their hearts.

Is there someone God is calling you to encourage today? Perhaps you're the one who needs an encouraging word. If you listen closely, perhaps you'll sense your heavenly Father cheering for you today.

⌐

Dear Lord, please make me an encourager who instills courage and confidence into the lives of others. Show me a brother or sister who needs a reassuring word today. In Jesus' name, amen.

ADDITIONAL SCRIPTURE READING:
1 CORINTHIANS 9:24-27; 2 TIMOTHY 4:7-8

78

Paul's Return...or Not

Our citizenship is in heaven. And we
eagerly await a Savior from there,
the Lord Jesus Christ, who, by the power that
enables him to bring everything
under his control, will transform our lowly bodies
so that they will be like his glorious body.

PHILIPPIANS 4:20-21

Fluffy, you were a naughty boy when you ran out in the street on Monday." The woman in front of me at the veterinarian's office scolded her cat as though it were a wayward child. She cocked her head as if listening and continued, "Oh, was it Tuesday?"

From the time our golden retriever was a pup, she has had trouble with dry, itchy skin, which required multiple visits to the veterinarian's office. One particular day she was scratching as much as she was breathing, so I decided to trek down to the doctor's office for some medication. The office was unusually busy, and the line at the checkout counter was five customers deep. I was the caboose.

There was one lady at the front of the line with a mountain lion of a cat who had everyone's undivided attention. The entire waiting room was staring wide-eyed as this woman carried on a one-way conversation with her feline. Then she turned to us and explained.

"Fluffy is the reincarnation of a deceased friend of mine. My good friend, Paul, passed away not too long ago. Then two days later, Fluffy appeared on my doorstep out of nowhere, and he has been with me ever since."

Then this woman encouraged us fellow pet owners to join in the conversation with her feline. The cat looked bored and regarded us as if we were mere subjects who should be honored to be in his presence. I decided my dog didn't really need medication after all and eased my way to the door.

Driving home, God assured me that He had plans for my after-life, and it did not involve being reincarnated into a cat, a cow, or any other furry beast. I was going to have a heavenly body that resembled Jesus Christ's...imperishable, incorruptible, and clothed in glory and honor. And He knew exactly where Paul was...and he was not at the veterinarian's office.

Do you ever think about heaven? Do you look forward to the day when there is no more pain, no more sorrow, and no more suffering? Today, let's praise God that we will be spending eternity in heaven with Him.

Heavenly Father, some days my earthly suit feels as though it is simply wearing out. Thank You that one day I will leave it behind and receive a heavenly body that will never get sick, never get tired, never grow old. In Jesus' name, amen.

ADDITIONAL SCRIPTURE READING:
1 JOHN 3:2-3; 1 CORINTHIANS 15:1-57

79

I Just Called to Say "I Love You"

I love you, O LORD, my strength.

PSALM 18:1

I t was a surprising phone call.

Steven was a sophomore in college, and he didn't call home as often as this mother's heart would have liked, but I was trying my best to let him go and grow. Steve and I had given him roots, and now it was time to give Steven wings. So I was delighted when I noticed his number on my caller ID.

"Hey, Mom. I just wanted to call and say hello. I haven't talked to you in a while, and I wanted to see how you were doing."

"Hey, bud," I replied. "How are you? How are your classes? Do you like your professors?"

We chatted about his classes and what he was learning. He caught me up on his roommate and various other students from our hometown. Then he asked me what I'd been up to, how the ministry was going, and what I'd been working on.

We got ready to say goodbye, and I said, "Wait a minute. Don't you need anything?"

"Nope. I just called to talk. Are you surprised?"

"Sort of," I sheepishly admitted. "But it is a wonderful surprise!"

After we said our goodbyes and "I love yous," I sat reveling in the joy of Steven's call. He hadn't called because he needed money for books, had a question about car insurance, or wanted help with a problem. He just called to talk...because he loved me.

Then God began to speak to my heart. *Sharon, I want you to remember how you feel at this moment. Your son, whom you love more than life itself, has just called to talk to you...not because He wanted anything, not because he had a question about a decision or a detail of life, not because he had a problem to solve. He called just to talk, simply to see what was on your heart—because he loves you. That, My child, whom I love more than life, is the same way I feel when you talk to Me—not because you want something, not because you have a question about a decision or a detail of life, not because you have a problem to solve. That is how I feel when you talk to Me simply because you want to learn what is on My heart…simply because you love Me.*

Today, let's tell God how much we love Him.

⌒

Dear Father, I love You. That's really all I want to say today. I love You, not because of what You do, but because of who You are…my heavenly Dad. In Jesus' name, amen.

ADDITIONAL SCRIPTURE READING: PSALM 138:1-8

80

A Healthy Dose of Perspective

This is the day the LORD has made;
let us rejoice and be glad in it.

PSALM 118:24

It was just a quick checkup at the doctor's office…or at least that's what it was supposed to be. My to-do list resembled a mile-long scroll and several deadlines loomed like a thundercloud ready to burst. But the appointment would take just a few minutes. Just enough time to catch my breath.

"Good morning, Mrs. Jaynes," the cheery receptionist greeted. "May I see your insurance card, please?"

We went through the regular check-in procedure, and then I settled in a comfy chair with a magazine that I would not normally have read. Because this was just a quick visit, I knew I wouldn't have time to read a full-length article. My, my. The trouble those Hollywood folks get into.

Ten minutes turned into fifteen, then into twenty, and then into thirty. My to-do list began growing heavier and heavier in my mind.

"Excuse me," I said, interrupting the receptionist. "My appointment was thirty minutes ago. Did they forget me?"

"I'm so sorry," she reassured me. "I'll check on it right away."

In just a few moments, a nurse appeared at the door. "Mrs. Jaynes, come right this way." My second stop was into a stark treatment room with more outdated magazines. The clock continued to tick. With each passing minute my frustration grew. "I'm glad he's not checking my blood pressure," I grumbled to no one in particular.

Fifty minutes after I had walked into the office for my quick five-minute checkup, the doctor himself walked into my room. My to-do list was magnified in my mind. My time was important too, you know. I didn't have time to sit around and read outdated gossip magazines!

The doctor was actually a friend of mine, but I was feeling less than friendly. *Ice sculpture* is a description that comes to mind when I think of my probable appearance.

"Hi, Sharon," he began. "I'm sorry you had to wait so long. I had to tell a patient she has terminal cancer. It took longer than I thought it would."

Tears pooled in my eyes, and my icy countenance melted into a puddle on the shiny tile floor. I was upset about not checking errands off my to-do list, and the woman in the next room was pondering how she was going to spend her last days on earth.

Yes, I did have a checkup that day. God was the doctor, and He looked into my heart to see that my perspective on life needed surgery. What's really important? My silly list of errands? No. What should be at the top of my to-do list today and every day is to celebrate each day as an incredible gift from God.

What is the Heart Doctor telling you today? What's at the top of your to-do list?

Dear God, thank You for another day of life. Sometimes I get so caught up in my little lists that I lose perspective of the true meaning of life. Help me to live my days glorifying You with every breath that I take and step that I make. In Jesus' name, amen.

ADDITIONAL SCRIPTURE READING: PSALM 118:1-29

81

God's Little Post-it Notes

Since the creation of the world, God's invisible qualities—
his eternal power and divine nature—have been clearly seen,
being understood from what has been made, so
that people are without excuse.

ROMANS 1:20 TNIV

I believe one of the greatest inventions of the twentieth century was the Post-it Note. First they were yellow. Then came fuchsia, turquoise, buttercup, and magenta. From full-page mega notes to tiny little strips, sticky notes have helped me compartmentalize and kept me organized. Mostly, they have served as visual reminders of information, events, and appointments not to forget.

But visual reminders that help us not to forget didn't begin with Post-it Notes. They began with God Himself. All through life God places His Post-it Notes on our days to remind us of Him. Just today I jotted down a few things God placed throughout my day:

- the sunrise with swirls of mist rising from the lake behind my home
- a vibrant red male cardinal and his demure wife sharing the bird feeder
- boisterous Canada geese flying in V-formation across the sky
- tulip leaves peeping through the ground
- dogwood blossoms heralding Easter's approach
- a weeping willow praising God in the breeze
- a monarch butterfly perched on the windowsill
- midday sunlight dancing on the water
- a baby's cry
- a little girl's giggle

- orange, magenta, and red streaks across the sky as the sun bids goodnight
- a sliver of white in the inky sky with a smattering of twinkles all around
- my husband's hand reaching for me in the night

Every one of these was God's reminder to me that He has infused my life with His presence. Through His creation, God longs for us to see and discover, observe and remember His creative beauty, His enduring grace, and His fathomless love.

In the Bible Paul wrote to the Romans, "Since the creation of the world, God's invisible qualities—his eternal power and divine nature—have been clearly seen, being understood from what has been made, so that people are without excuse" (Romans 1:20 TNIV). If we do not hear from God today, if we do not see His fingerprints through creation, we are without excuse. He *is* speaking to us all day long with holy Post-it Notes to remind us of His presence in our lives. The question is, will we listen?

Today, consider making a list of holy Post-it Notes God has scattered throughout your day.

Dear God, thank You for the little reminders You place on the moments of my days. Help me not to miss them, but to see the many love notes from You. In Jesus' name, amen.

ADDITIONAL SCRIPTURE READING:
PSALM 19:1-6; PSALM 96:1-13

82

Hand in Hand

Two are better than one because they have
a good return for their labor.
For if either of them falls, the one will lift up his companion.
But woe to the one who falls when there
is not another to lift him up...
A cord of three strands is not quickly torn apart.

ECCLESIASTES 4:9-10,12 NASB

Looking out my den window, I noticed two of my neighbors slowly walking down the street. Ernestine, with her bald head snuggled in a woolen cap, held tightly to Patti's supporting arm. Patti's chestnut hair, just two inches long, shone like a victor's crown—the crown of a cancer survivor.

One May, Patti felt a lump and feared the worst. A doctor's visit confirmed that she had cancer. For three months she endured chemotherapy, which was followed by seven weeks of radiation five days a week. As God would have it, her final treatment fell on Thanksgiving Day. Yes, she had much to be thankful for—a full life, a loving husband, and Ernestine, her next-door neighbor.

When Ernestine moved into the neighborhood two years before, she and Patti connected as if they had known each other all their lives. Patti said, "Even though Ernestine is only fifteen years my senior, I feel as if God has given me the gift of another mother."

During Patti's cancer treatments, Ernestine was right by her side, an extension of Jesus' hands and feet providing love, encouragement, and support. By July of that year, Patti had lost all her hair, and Ernestine was the one person, besides Patti's husband, with whom she felt comfortable not wearing her wig.

One year after her final radiation treatment, Patti was given the opportunity to return the kindness to Ernestine. A trip to the doctor revealed that Ernestine had lymphoma, cancer of the lymph nodes.

Now Patti was the nurturer. She took Ernestine to her first chemother-apy session and explained what to expect. She told Ernestine what to eat, where to have a wig made, and how to deal with depression.

"I never had to tell Patti what I needed," Ernestine remembered, "because she already knew, sometimes when I didn't even know myself. She'd say, 'Ernestine, I think you need to take a little walk. It'll make you feel better.' Now, if someone else had told me that, I might have said, 'Leave me alone. You don't know how I feel.' But Patti did know how I felt. She'd traveled the road just a few months before. I know beyond a shadow of a doubt that God moved me here, right next door to Patti. He is good."

As I watched the twosome make their way down the street that chilly November day, I whispered a prayer, thanking God for girl-friends in God...friends who can be His hands and feet when one is too weak to walk unassisted, His strong arm when a burden is too heavy to bear alone, and His voice when we have forgotten the words to the song in our heart.

Today, ask God if there is someone to whom you can be an exten-sion of His strong arm.

Dear God, thank You that I don't have to go through life alone. Thank You for friends who have kept me from falling and friends who picked me up when I did. Show me someone I can lift up today. In Jesus' name, amen.

ADDITIONAL SCRIPTURE READING:
2 CORINTHIANS 1:2-11; EPHESIANS 4:1-6,32

83

What's Wrong with This Thing?

*"Not by might nor by power, but by
my Spirit," says the LORD Almighty.*

ZECHARIAH 4:6

I t was the incompetent and the inexperienced being led by the
inept—the day our Sunday school class worked on the Habitat for
Humanity house for an unsuspecting, extremely grateful Vietnamese
family. Among the crew were two dentists, an investment banker, a
lawyer, an engineer, two pastors, a receptionist, several homemakers,
and a marriage counselor. (It's always good to have a marriage counselor on hand when a home improvement project is taking place.)

The thousand-square-foot vinyl-siding house had already been
framed by a team the week before. Today was drywall day. The site
supervisor's name was TA. That's all the information he gave—just TA.
TA became a Christian one Easter when he reluctantly agreed to go
to church with his praying wife. He was a country carpenter who had
hammered more nails for Jesus than Noah and his sons put together.

My friend Palmer was part of the drywall team. Like Rambo, he
wielded his screw gun and popped those babies in the drywall like a hot
knife through butter. Piece of cake. After several hours of neck-craning,
screw-popping, dust-in-your-eyes labor, Palmer took a 15-minute
break.

Reenergized, Rambo picked up his machine gun and once again
attacked the ceiling. A lot of forgetting can go on in a 15-minute break
and for some reason the screws forgot how they were supposed to spin
out of the gun and magically implant flush with the ceiling.

That's strange, Palmer thought as he examined the screw protruding
one inch from the ceiling.

He moved the gun over a couple of inches and tried again. *Maybe
I just need to push harder*, he decided. So with all the force of a trained

counselor, Palmer pressed the gun into the ceiling and pulled the trigger. Once again the screw hung down one inch from the ceiling.

Like a tennis player who examines his racket after missing an easy lob, or an outfielder who stares at his glove after missing a simple fly ball, Palmer looked at the gun in frustration. "Something is definitely wrong with this gun," he mumbled. "I guess I need to push even harder." Palmer set his jaw, gripped the gun, and firmly pressed the screw gun into the ceiling. "I'm a man. I can do this. I'm going to make this work."

After a third attempt, a frustrated Palmer stared at a neatly placed row of three taunting screws protruding from the ceiling. About that time, TA bounced through the room and casually commented, "Hey, buddy, you might want to take that gun out of reverse."

A flush of embarrassment rose from the tip of Palmer's dusty shoes to the top of his sandy-blond head. He nonchalantly flipped the switch to forward and proceeded shooting flush screws efficiently and effectively as though nothing had ever happened.

Later, Palmer laughingly said, "Sometimes I'm not the brightest person in the world, but I wonder how many rows of protruding screws I would have shot into that ceiling before I stopped and even considered that the problem might be me?"

Okay, sisters, stop the cameras. Suddenly I saw myself staring up at those protruding screws with my baffled friend. "What's wrong with her?" I whine about someone who's let me down. "What's wrong with him?" I complain about my husband, who's not acting according to my plan. "What's wrong with them?" I mumble about family members who are not living up to my expectations. In frustration I continue repeating the same ineffective behavior, never stopping to consider the problem might be me.

As I pondered Palmer's dilemma, I considered a few of my own. Hmm. In my struggles of life, could the problem be…me? Am I the one that needs to make a change? Do I need to put a certain area of my life in reverse? Do I need to turn and go in the opposite direction?

Interestingly, the word "repentance" means "to turn and go in the opposite direction." So let me ask that question again. Do I need to repent in a certain area of my life?

If life isn't working for you, consult with the project manager—Jesus Christ. Maybe you need to hit the reverse switch in your own life.

Dear Heavenly Father, sometimes I try harder, but with the same results. I repeat the same ineffective behavior and then wonder why I don't have more victory in my life. Show me when I need to turn and go in the opposite direction, and give me the courage to do so. In Jesus' name, amen.

ADDITIONAL SCRIPTURE READING: JAMES 1:1-15

84

It's Not Over Till It's Over

*Thanks be to God! He gives us the victory
through our Lord Jesus Christ.*

1 CORINTHIANS 15:57

I t's called "March Madness," and in the Jaynes' home, it is important…at least to some of us. It was Friday night, and my family and
I were rooting for the University of North Carolina at Chapel Hill Tar
Heels as they took on Southern California in the NCAA basketball
tournament. All three of us had graduated from UNC, and we were
pulling for the Tar Heels, but it wasn't looking too good for the home
team. Partway through the game, we decided to play a game of Scrabble to augment the excitement. By the end of the first half, we were
down by 16 points.

"We're going to lose," we agreed.

"It's not worth staying up for," Steve said. "It's late. I'm tired, and
they look tired too. I don't want to watch them get creamed. They'll
never come back from 16 points."

So we finished our Scrabble game, turned off the television, and
said our goodnights.

You can imagine our surprise Saturday morning when we opened
the newspaper to read the headlines: "It's a Tar Heel Blitz!" They had
come from behind to win the game.

The coach must have had a powerful pep talk at the half, because
the Tar Heels came back "crashing to the offensive boards" coupled
with a "suffocating defense." Southern Cal's 16-point lead became 10,
then 6, then 3, and suddenly UNC had the lead. Once they had it, they
wouldn't let it go. They scored 18 straight points and eventually won,
74 to 64. What an exciting game! And we missed it.

I could almost hear God in the background. *See, you quit too soon…
again.*

Sometimes when we're struggling in life and it looks as though we're going to lose, we turn off the game and go to bed. We quit too soon. But just because it looks as though we're losing doesn't mean we are. The game's not over! God is still at work, and if we give up, we'll miss the thrill of victory.

If you are going through a difficult time right now, and you feel that the situation is hopeless, be encouraged…don't give up! It's not over till it's over and we're hearing the "Hallelujah" chorus as we pass those pearly gates. God is always at work. I don't know about you, but I don't want to miss a single moment of the miraculous win.

⌐

Dear Lord, forgive me for giving up too soon. I pray that my faith will remain strong in all situations. Even if I can't see You at work, I know You are. Thank You that we are more than conquerors through Christ Jesus. In Jesus' name, amen.

ADDITIONAL SCRIPTURE READING:
REVELATION 2:7,11,17,26; 3:5,12,21; 21:7

85

Who Knew?

To Him who is able to do far more abundantly
beyond all that we ask or think,
according to the power that works within
us, to Him be the glory in the church
and in Christ Jesus to all generations forever and ever. Amen.

EPHESIANS 3:20-21 NASB

How could we have been so wrong? We thought we heard from God. Where did we miss it?

These questions plagued my husband and me after an important life decision seemed to fall apart.

When Steve was in his last year of graduate school, we prayed fervently for the Lord to show us where He would have us set up Steve's dental practice. Dentists tend to start a practice in one city and never leave. There are no job transfers, and the corporate office doesn't change locations. So we knew this was somewhat of a permanent decision.

I wanted a vision from the Lord, a star in the east, or handwriting on the wall. Of course, I never received any such sign. Most of the time those listening to God do not. But we sought wise counsel, prayed for direction, and explored several options. Finally, we felt the Lord was leading us to Charlotte, North Carolina. There was an older dentist in town who was looking for a young upstart to come in and take over some of his patient load. It was not a good part of town, and not exactly what we would have chosen, but this doctor had too many patients and we didn't have any, so we thought it would be a perfect fit.

One week after we had moved from Chapel Hill to Charlotte, set up housekeeping, and started our new life, the doctor called Steve into his office for a little chat. "Son," he said "I've decided I don't want to have another dentist in the office after all. Sorry for any inconvenience. See ya later and good luck." He shook Steve's hand and walked out of the room.

After a year of seeking God's will, searching for where He wanted us to live the rest of our days, and moving to Charlotte, it was "sorry" and "good luck."

"Lord," we cried, "how could we have been so wrong? How could we have heard You so poorly?" Considering the bleakness of the situation, we concluded that we had made a terrible mistake.

For three months we worked in one office on Fridays and Saturdays. Then I worked in another office on Mondays through Thursdays. Our saying was, "Sharon works six days a week and cries on the seventh." This was not fun.

A few months later, one of the best dentists in town invited Steve to come to his office, rent one room as an operatory, and share the common spaces, such as x-ray darkroom and waiting room. So off we went, to the most desirable part of town, to one of the best practices in Charlotte, where we stayed for two years—just enough time to sink our roots deep in the red North Carolina soil. On the third year, we had enough money saved to branch out on our own without sinking in debt.

Thirty years later, Steve has an incredible practice, which God has richly blessed. God's plans were exceeding abundantly more than we could have ever asked or thought. Had the original situation not fallen apart, we would not have been available for God's best when it became available.

Who knew? God did.

All through life God opens and closes doors. Sometimes we move forward, sure we have heard from Him. And sometimes those situations fall apart. Then we ask, "Did I hear God right? How could I have been so wrong?"

But just because circumstances don't work out as we thought they would does not mean we didn't hear God correctly. He is much more interested in the process than in the finished product. The closed door could be part of the journey He had planned all along. Is it confusing? Yes. Is it difficult? Usually. Will we understand? Not always.

Is there a situation in your life that has seemingly fallen apart? Rather than saying "Why me?" how about saying "What now?" Let's approach today and every day with open ears to hear, open eyes to see, and open hearts to trust wherever He leads.

What will today hold? Who knows? God knows.

⌒

Father, no matter what happens in my life today, I know You are Sovereign. Help me not to panic when things don't go as I have planned, but to rest in the assurance that You have everything under control. In Jesus' name, amen.

ADDITIONAL SCRIPTURE READING:
ROMANS 8:28-29; ISAIAH 55:8-9

86

Divine Appointment

Jesus said, "Take care of my sheep."

JOHN 21:16

To Beth, it was the confusion of an inept airline. To me, it was a divine appointment from God.

"I don't have an assigned seat," the disheveled young woman complained as she stumbled onto the airplane.

"This one is empty," I pointed out.

"Thanks," she huffed as she plopped down in the seat next to me.

The beautiful young lady was obviously exhausted. She was dressed in skintight jeans, and a low-cut T-shirt. Her flip-flops slid under her feet to reveal a tattoo on the top of her foot. Sunglasses hid something...I wasn't sure what. She looked straight ahead, but I felt that her mind was traveling to a distant place.

After the plane left the ground, I pulled out my latest book, which I was reviewing for an upcoming radio interview. *Put the book down and talk to this girl*, God seemed to say.

God, she doesn't want to talk. I can tell by her body language. She's not interested in conversation, I mentally argued.

Put the book down and talk to this girl. (God can be very persistent. Especially when it comes to one of His little lost lambs.)

I closed the book and turned to this...kid.

"So, where are you headed?" I asked.

"Home," she replied.

"Where's home?"

"Right outside of Charlotte," she replied. "It's a small town. I'm sure you've never heard of it."

"Were you in Florida on business or pleasure?" I continued.

"I was visiting my boyfriend."

Then she took off her sunglasses to reveal swollen red eyes. She glanced down at the book in my lap. *"Your Scars Are Beautiful to God,"* she read. "That's an interesting topic. I've got lots of scars."

"So do I," I replied. "That's why I wrote the book."

"You wrote that book?"

"Yep."

For the next hour and a half she poured out her heart. She had been abandoned by her birth father and sexually abused by several men in her life. She was on this flight home because her boyfriend, who had just come out of a drug rehabilitation center, had "roughed her up." Actually, she was fleeing. My heart broke as this beautiful young girl told me story after story of cruelties that had been done *to* her mingled with bad choices that had been made *through* her. At the moment, her life resembled a train wreck with one lone survivor who was in desperate need of life resuscitation.

As my mind engaged with Beth (not her real name), my spirit communed with God. *What do I do? So much hurt. So much pain.*

Pray for her…now.

"Beth, would you mind if I prayed for you?"

"No," she said with a quiver in her voice. "I'd like that."

I held her hand and God's sorrow for this girl filled my heart. It wasn't just a "God bless Beth," sort of prayer. I sobbed. It was as if God's pain for this girl I didn't even know was flowing through me.

As He would have it, Beth and I were on the front row of the plane. The only person paying any attention to us was the flight attendant who sat facing us in her jump seat. I'm not sure, but I think God was working in her heart as well.

When the plane landed, I handed Beth the book, we exchanged e-mail addresses, and embraced one last time. Since then we have kept in touch, and Beth has continued her journey for peace and purpose. Her stepfather wrote me a letter expressing his appreciation for taking the time to minister to his "little girl." He wrote: "I had been praying for God to send Beth an angel, and I believe He did."

Well, I'm no angel, that's for sure, but I believe angels were hovering around us in that plane. And for one young lady and one not-so-young woman, God moved in a powerful way.

Throughout life, God will prompt us to pray, lend a helping hand, or offer a word of encouragement. Will we listen? Will be obey? The answer to those two questions can change the course of someone's life.

⌒

Dear Father, help me to detect Your still, small voice and obey
Your gentle nudges. Give me the courage and the confidence to
reach out and take care of Your sheep today. In Jesus' name, amen.

ADDITIONAL SCRIPTURE READING: ACTS 8:26-40

87

It Was a Dark and Stormy Night

Our light and momentary troubles are achieving for us
an eternal glory that far outweighs them all. So we fix
our eyes not on what is seen, but on what is unseen. For
what is seen is temporary, but what is unseen is eternal.

2 CORINTHIANS 4:17-18

Up at 4:30 a.m., I was preparing to speak at a Good Friday prayer breakfast in Oil City, Pennsylvania. At the event the Holy Spirit showed up, God moved in, and we had a great beginning to a wonderful weekend celebrating Christ's resurrection.

After the event it was off to the Philadelphia airport for a quick one-and-a-half-hour flight home. Easter weekend had the airport teeming with travelers. As we waited, clouds began to roll in and planes failed to roll out. Unfortunately, overbooked airplanes and stormy weather do not a good combination make. Delays and cancellations lit up the departure board.

I was scheduled to arrive in Charlotte at 7:00 p.m. But then my arrival time was pushed back to 7:40, then to 8:40, then to 9:30. This was turning out to be not such a good Friday after all. Travelers were getting angry, ticketing agents were getting agitated, and kids were getting antsy. I just wanted to go home.

Finally, after gate changes and time delays, we boarded the plane headed for Charlotte. As we neared North Carolina, the pilot made an announcement. "Unfortunately, the storm is passing through Charlotte at this time and we will not be able to land. We are going to land in Greensboro, 90 miles away, and wait it out. Feel free to disembark the airplane, but do not leave the boarding area. We will make an announcement when it is time to reboard. Don't worry. We'll get you to Charlotte just as quickly as possible. Sorry for the inconvenience."

Arg. We landed in Greensboro and waited...and waited...and waited. About 10:30, there was another announcement. "May I have your attention please? For those traveling on flight 389 to Charlotte, unfortunately the flight crew has logged in too many hours and will not be able to continue the flight to Charlotte. We have secured vans to drive you the rest of the way. Sorry for the inconvenience."

A collective moan rose from the motley bunch. We trudged down to baggage claim, retrieved our bags, and separated into groups of nine.

"What do you do?" a man in a business suit asked, trying to pass the time.

"I'd rather not say," I answered. Thinking he might get the wrong idea, I smiled and said, "Just kidding. I'm an author."

"What do you write?"

I was hoping he wouldn't ask me that. I was not being a very good advertisement just then. "I write Christian-oriented books for women," I answered. "You know, the kind that tells women how to handle difficulties in life." We all started laughing.

We piled into the van: eight traveling to visit family, one going home. The air-conditioner was broken, and heat blew out of the vents in every direction. No one could figure out how to shut it down. Temperatures rose, sweat poured, layers came off, the windows fogged up. It was miserable.

After about an hour and a half, I started to relax, thinking we would be in Charlotte any minute. In the seat in front of me, a twentysomething woman and her mother chatted happily. They were on their way to spend the weekend with daughter number two. Daughter number one, who was apparently tracking our progress on her iPhone, turned around in her seat to face me.

"We're passing Statesville," she said. "How much farther do we have?"

"Statesville!" I cried. "We're not supposed to be passing Statesville! He's going the wrong way!"

Our one-and-a-half-hour van ride turned into a three-hour van ride. This was just the icing on a very bad cake. I had way too much material for a new book on suffering and was ready for this not-so-good Friday to be over. Just as I was having a not-so-nice, one-way conversation with God, the mother in front of me drew a smiley face on the window. A smiley face!

What in the world does she have to be happy about! I mused. *I don't see anything "smiley" about this entire situation!*

We finally arrived in Charlotte after midnight. The one-and-a-half-hour trip had turned into an eight-hour nightmare. Nine dripping wet, exhausted passengers climbed out of the van and breathed in the fresh night air.

"Bye, Stephanie," I said to the young iPhone-toting girl. "You have fun with your sister and mom this weekend."

"Oh, we will," she replied. "My mom just found out that she has cancer for the second time. It doesn't look too good. We're going to spend a weekend together, just the three of us, simply enjoying each other."

She turned to walk away...never seeing the tears that filled my eyes.

I looked back at the van's window that still held the picture of a smiley face drawn by a dying woman's hand. Suddenly, my night of little inconveniences seemed rather petty. It was a Good Friday after all. God reminded me of all I had to be thankful for. Storms will come in this life. It is our perspective in the storm that will determine whether we will grumble and complain or draw a smiley face and thank God for each and every breath we have.

I slipped into the car with my precious, patient husband, gave him a quick kiss, and drew a smiley face on the window.

⌣

Dear Lord, forgive me when I whine over life's inconveniences.
In the storms of life, help me see Your blessings in the
raindrops, Your power in the lightning, and Your
voice in the rolling thunder. In Jesus' name, amen.

Additional Scripture Reading: Acts 16:16-31

88

Taking the Good with the Bad

We urge you, brothers, warn those who are idle,
encourage the timid, help the weak, be patient with everyone.

1 THESSALONIANS 5:14

As I sat on my screened-in porch early one spring morning, I was taken aback with the beauty surrounding me. A layer of mist rose from the serene waters of the lake and hovered just above the surface. Rays of light slanting in from the east elongated shadows that all too soon would stand at attention in the noonday sun. Pampas grass plumes praised their Creator with a gentle sway.

I held a steamy cup of coffee in my hand and placed my Bible on my lap. As if on cue, as had been our routine for the past several weeks, a visitor hopped from the shrubbery and onto the night-cooled patio. "Good morning, Peter," I cooed to the little brown bunny I'd watched grow since early spring. "And how are you today?" *I just love bunnies,* I mused.

Peter skipped and jumped from bush to bush, and kicked up his heels like an Irishman ready to meet the day. As usual, he stopped right in front of the porch and blinked his big brown eyes as if to say hello. Just as I was enjoying watching my furry friend, he hopped over to a flower pot, stood up on his hind legs, and yanked a rather large stem of petunia from the plant.

"Good grief," I moaned. "Stop that!" Bounding down the steps, I came face-to-face with the wrascally wrabbit. "Stop eating my flowers," I warned. "Get out of here. Shoo."

Apparently, the bunny didn't see me as much of a threat. He didn't budge, but continued munching away. I could have touched him if I'd wanted.

"I mean it," I continued. "Shoo." It wasn't until I clapped my hands several times that Peter scampered behind the bush to finish up his breakfast.

Back on the porch, I grabbed my lukewarm coffee and placed my Bible back on my lap. It wasn't long before a dainty hummingbird buzzed up to the hummingbird feeder just outside the screen. I watched in amazement as its wings fluttered and it hovered in mid-air. Iridescent colors of green and blue glistened in the sun. "I just love hummingbirds," I whispered.

No sooner had the thought entered my head than a second hummingbird dive-bombed the first. A fight quickly ensued. Beak to beak, they battled for their terrain. Right jab. Left stab. "Guys, stop it," I pled as if they cared. "There are six perches and enough nectar for the entire country. Good grief!" And as quickly as they had appeared, they were gone.

Taking a sip from my now cold coffee, I tried once again to concentrate on my open Bible. But then I saw our heron approaching. A beautiful heron lives on our lake and occasionally he passes our way. I marveled at his long legs pointing behind him and his slender beak leading the way. With exaggerated movements, he slowly flapped his magnificent blue-gray wings and glided before me. But then, like a Boeing 747 with a leak in the fuselage, a stream of poo fell from the bird and made a trail in the yard.

"Good grief," I moaned for the third time in one day.

Back to the Bible. As I tried to concentrate, God began speaking to my heart about what I had seen. *Are you willing to take the good with the bad?* He seemed to say.

"What do You mean, Lord?" I questioned.

You love bunnies, but they eat your plants. You love hummingbirds, but they constantly fight. You love the heron, but he makes a mess in your yard. Are you willing to take the good with the bad?

"Well, yes. I am willing to take the good with the bad. I love Your creatures!"

What about people? He seemed to continue. *If you are willing to take the good with the bad with mere animals, are you willing to take the good with the bad in people created in My image?*

"That's not funny, God," I argued.

It's not meant to be.

And then, as God so often does in my life, He left me to think about it. I began to think about people in my life I have rejected or relationships I have walked away from because of annoying behavior or emotional messiness. It seems I was willing to take the good with the bad with God's furry feathery creatures, but when it came to people created in God's image...not so much.

God is a Master at taking the good with the bad, whether dealing with David the adulterer, Jacob the liar, Peter the doubter, or the woman I look at in the mirror every day. God sees the best and the worst in others and loves them just the same.

So here's the question for us today. Are we willing to take the good with the bad? Are we willing to overlook the annoying behavior of others and embrace their positive qualities instead? I'm going to leave you to think about it the way God left me to think about it that particular morning.

Heavenly Father, all I can say today is HELP! Help me be patient, loving, and kind. Help me to focus on the positives of others and shrug off the negatives. And, Lord, help others do the same with me. In Jesus' name, amen.

ADDITIONAL SCRIPTURE READING: MATTHEW 18:23-35

89

A Simple Gesture

Encourage one another daily, as long as it is called Today.

HEBREWS 3:13

It seemed as though my husband was always pumping gas. Living out in the country and driving into town each day requires a lot of gas. One day as he stood holding the nozzle and watching the numbers rapidly roll by higher and higher, he noticed an old Honda Civic pull up to the pump behind him. The car had seen better days. It had a rusted roof, missing hubcaps, faded paint, and a dented bumper.

Out of the corner of his eye he observed a young woman who appeared to be in her late twenties get out of the car. She was dressed in medical scrubs and looked about as tired as her Civic. Methodically, she swiped her card, placed the nozzle in the tank, and squeezed the handle. After a few seconds, she stopped squeezing. She then placed the nozzle back in the pump and began screwing the cap back on her tank.

That couldn't have been more than a couple of gallons, Steve thought. "Is that all the gas you're getting?" he asked.

"Yeah, well, you know. Trying to space it out," she replied.

Steve placed his nozzle back in its holder, walked over to her pump, and swiped his card. "Let's fill it up today."

"No, no. You can't do that," she protested.

"I already did," he smiled. "It's already done. See. The card's approved. Fill it up."

Tears welled up in her eyes. "Thank you," she said.

"You have a good day," he replied. "God bless." And off he drove.

I just love that man.

As I thought about Steve's act of kindness, I was challenged to pay closer attention to those around me throughout my busy days. I was stirred to look for someone who needed a kind word, a bill paid, a burden carried.

Throughout the 33 years Jesus walked this earth, He noticed people who crossed His path during *His* busy day. He noticed a small man in a tree straining to catch a glimpse as He passed by (Luke 19:1-10). He noticed a woman with a bent-over back sitting in the women's section of the synagogue straining to hear (Luke 13:10-17). He noticed a lame man who had been sitting by a pool for 38 years (John 5:1-8). He noticed a grieving mother mourning the loss of her only son (Luke 7:11-14). He noticed the hunger of the crowd after a long day of teaching on the hillside (Mark 6:30-44). He noticed…and He did something about it.

It is very easy to go about our busy days with blinders on—focusing on our own little worlds and ignoring the ministry opportunities surrounding us. But Jesus showed us how to pay attention, lighten a load, bestow a blessing, give a gift, help the hurting, and bind up the brokenhearted.

Jesus was busy! He had a lot to accomplish in the three-and-a-half years of His earthly ministry. But He was never *too* busy to notice the needs of the people around Him and to obey His Father's nudges to help.

Steve was my hero that day. And I suspect, for one young lady in a beat-up Honda Civic, he was her hero as well. Whose hero will you be today?

⌣

Dear Lord, open my eyes today. Forgive me for being
so selfish that I forget to notice the needs all around
me. Show me someone I can help today. Show me how
I can be Your hands and feet today. I'm listening. I'm
watching. I'm paying attention. In Jesus' name, amen.

ADDITIONAL SCRIPTURE READING: MATTHEW 25:31-45

90

Tearing Up the Scorecards

Love is patient, love is kind...it is not self-seeking,
it is not easily angered, it keeps no record of wrongs.

1 CORINTHIANS 13:4-5

She was at it again. Mrs. Barnett was getting out the scorecards and tallying up the points.

I sat with an older woman as she began enumerating her family's shortcomings. "Callie never comes to see me," she began to complain about her granddaughter. "And she never calls me, either. I saw her sitting on the other side of the church last week, and she didn't even come over and give me a hug."

Throughout our time together, Mrs. Barnett mentioned several family members and friends who had disappointed her, who had not lived up to her expectations, and who had not given her the love she felt she deserved. The more I listened, the clearer a picture began to take shape in my mind. I envisioned Mrs. Barnett with a big stack of mental scorecards. At the top of each card was a name: a grandchild, a child, a friend, a pastor, and, yes, even one with my name printed across the top. Each person had points added or subtracted from their cards according to how much or how little attention they gave her.

Friend, let me tell you a great life lesson. As long as this woman keeps mental scorecards on the people in her life, she is going to be miserable. And if you or I keep scorecards for the people in our lives, we will be miserable as well.

Love is about giving—not necessarily about giving money or gifts, but giving love. Can I say that again? Love is about giving love. Love does not keep records of wrongs or perceived wrongs. It does not involve an accounting tally sheet of debits and credits or scorecards of plusses and minuses. It does not keep a running list of kindnesses to reward those who come out on top and shun those who do not.

With genuine love, there are no scorecards. I'm certainly glad God tore up mine long ago. David wrote, "If you, O LORD, kept a record of sin, O Lord, who could stand?" (Psalm 130:3). Certainly not me! If God doesn't keep a scorecard, making notes of the ways I have offended Him, disappointed Him, or not given Him the attention He deserves, then why do I think I have the right to keep scorecards on the people in my little world? He doesn't give plusses and minuses and then tally up our cards to see whether or not we deserve His love. God gives and gives and gives, and gets very little in return. Why does He do that? Because He loves you and me perfectly, wholly, and unconditionally.

Scorecards. Do you keep them? Do you keep mental lists of what people do and don't do to deserve your love? If so, you'll never be content or at peace in your relationships. No one may see the scorecards sitting on your coffee table, but they'll know they are there. They will see them in your eyes, hear them in your tone, and sense them in your touch. Let's pray and ask God to show us if we are keeping mental scorecards and then agree together to tear them up.

⌒

*Dear Lord, I am no longer going to keep a scorecard
for _____. Help me love the way You love—
unconditionally, with no strings attached. Help me to be thankful
for the attention I do receive rather than resentful for what I don't.
I do not want to become a bitter old woman people avoid,
but a grateful, graceful lady people enjoy. And, Lord,
whenever I begin to fall into the old habit of making mental notes
of how someone did not live up to my expectations,
I pray You will convict me and help me to replace the negative
thoughts with a prayer of thanksgiving. In Jesus' name, amen.*

ADDITIONAL SCRIPTURE READING:
1 CORINTHIANS 12:31–13:13

91

The Key to Freedom

It is for freedom that Christ has set us free. Stand firm, then,
and do not let yourselves be burdened again by a yoke of slavery.

GALATIANS 5:1

North Carolina has birthed some very influential men and women. Perhaps one of our favorites is Andy Griffith of the *Andy Griffith Show*. In Andy's fictional town of Mayberry, where Sheriff Andy Taylor patrolled, lived a town drunk named Otis Campbell. When Otis was arrested for public drunkenness, Andy put him a jail cell until he sobered up. Usually Andy's Aunt Bea cooked Otis a good meal during his stay. He even had his own cell—the one on the right. After a good night's sleep, if Otis woke up before Andy arrived at work the next morning, Otis would simply stick his hand through the bars of the jail cell door, take the key from a nail hanging on the wall, and let himself out. It was just that simple. On a few occasions, a drunken Otis stumbled into the jail late at night, locked himself in his cell, and placed the key back on the nail.

This was always a comical scene, but it reminds me of the jail we lock ourselves in when we remain a prisoner to our past. God has set us free, but sometimes *we lock ourselves up* in the prison of shame and guilt. Our key to freedom isn't hanging by a nail on a jailhouse wall, but hung by nails on a rugged cross. His name is Jesus. He came to set the prisoner free…for good. The key is always in reach and we never have to be locked up in the prison of shame and guilt again.

If you have locked yourself away in a jail cell of fear and doubt, shame and condemnation, or guilt and regret, know this…Jesus came to set you free, but you still have to make the choice to walk out that prison door. The truth is, you are deeply loved, completely forgiven, fully pleasing, and totally accepted by God.

Are you walking in freedom today? If not, the door is wide open and Jesus is waiting for you on the other side.

⌣

Dear Heavenly Father, thank You for setting me free!
Please forgive me when I slink back into the jail cell
of shame and guilt. I know You paid an incredible
price for my freedom, and it dishonors You when I do
not walk in that freedom. In Jesus' name, amen.

ADDITIONAL SCRIPTURE READING:
GALATIANS 5:1; JOHN 8:31-36

92

No More Shame

*I delight greatly in the LORD; my soul rejoices in my God. For
he has clothed me with garments of salvation and arrayed me
in a robe of righteousness, as a bridegroom adorns his head
like a priest, and as a bride adorns herself with her jewels.*

ISAIAH 61:10

Debbie's paternal grandparents had both a housekeeper and
groundskeeper who lived in their basement apartment. Nina and
Silas were like part of the family and had lived with the grandparents
for as long as Debbie could remember. On many occasions, when Debbie's parents and grandparents went out to dinner, she and her older sister were left in the care of Silas and Nina. The girls' parents had no idea
that Silas was molesting their precious children time and time again.

From the time Debbie and Beth were three and six years old, until
they were ten and thirteen, Silas fondled and sexually molested the
girls in the basement apartment lit only by the black-and-white television blinking in the background. While Silas ravaged Debbie's body,
her sister held her face in her hands and told her stories. Together, the
girls escaped to a land faraway while the worse nightmare imaginable
was played out before them.

Silas warned them, "If you tell anybody, I'll hurt your brother." So
the girls suffered in silence.

When Debbie was ten years old, she and her sister spent the night
with her maternal grandmother while her parents were away on a business trip. The elderly grandmother paused at the opened door to watch
her precious granddaughters kneeling beside their bed. With arms
wrapped around each other they began to say their prayers.

"Dear God, thank You for Mommy and Daddy and Kevin, and
Grandma and Grandpa Wilson, and Grandma James. We pray You
will protect us from Silas and keep him from hurting us and touching
us in private places. We pray…"

The stunned grandmother clutched her heart, rushed to embrace the girls, and sobbed uncontrollably. The rest was a blur.

A few hours later, in the wee hours of the morning, their parents came back from their business trip...two days early. The girls could hear their parents crying in the next room, but nothing was ever mentioned about Silas. All they knew was that the next time they went to Grandma and Grandpa Wilson's house, Silas and Nina were gone.

Years passed with little mention of the years of abuse by Silas. Like old war veterans who never mention the horrors of battle, the girls never mentioned the molestation again. However, the chronic pain of the past was an undercurrent to their total existence. Debbie felt dirty, used, and cheap. She felt like damaged goods.

Debbie accepted Jesus Christ as her Savior when she was a small child, but she had a difficult time believing Jesus could accept her. She didn't see herself as a precious holy child of God dressed in robes of righteousness. She saw herself as a dirty orphan dressed in tattered rags. Then one day, she went to a Bible study and heard for the first time about her identity as a child of God.

"I didn't feel like a holy child of God, but that's who the Bible said I was," she explained. "I read and reread that list of who I am in Christ. The more I studied about my new identity and the truth that sets us free, the more I began to accept it as true. I began to realize it was Satan who held up the picture of Silas and what he had done to me to remind me of who he wanted me to believe I was. But that was a lie. God took the truth and massaged it into my broken heart like a healing ointment. He placed a crown of beauty on my head and washed away the ashes. He gave me the oil of gladness instead of mourning, and dressed me in a garment of praise instead of despair. No longer was my identity determined by what happened to me as a child. My identity is determined by what happened in me through Jesus Christ."

Debbie accepted her new identity. It was there all along, like a cloak waiting to be placed on the princess' regal shoulders. She received the robe of righteousness and now walks with the confidence of a dearly loved child of the King.

This devotion may have been difficult for you to read, but it is very important. No matter what you have been through, if you know Jesus as Savior and Lord, you are a pure and holy child of the King.

Have you accepted your new identity? Are you ready to start believing the truth? Are you ready to put off the ragged robes of shame and put on the robe of righteousness that Jesus purchased just for you with His own life? He's holding it open for you right now. Slip it on. It's just your size.

Dear Heavenly Father who loves me, I come to You with a heart humbled by Your tender love for me. I thank You that You have removed the filthy rags of this world from my life and clothed me with the righteousness of Christ. Help me to hold my head high as a child of the King. In Jesus' name, amen.

ADDITIONAL SCRIPTURE READING: JOHN 8:1-11

93

Back Side of the Island

Why are you downcast, O my soul? Why so
disturbed within me? Put your hope in God, for I
will yet praise him, my Savior and my God.

PSALM 42:11

The cruise ship docked at Cozumel Island. My husband and I walked off the plank into the hustle and bustle of locals waiting to entertain the new batch of tourists entering their bit of paradise.

"Let's get away from all the congestion," Steve suggested. "I want to see the unspoiled part of the island."

So we rented a small motorcycle, donned our helmets, and set out on an adventure.

"This road goes around the island," the man who rented the bikes to us explained. "Just stay on this road and you will return."

Off we went to circle the beautiful island of Cozumel. It wasn't long before civilization lay behind and the open road promised romantic scenery. White sandy beaches hugged the road on the right. But after several miles, the landscaped changed. Lush palms transformed into bare craggy branches, seagulls were replaced with dark menacing vultures, and the terrain was piled high with garbage. We were lone travelers on the back side of the island, and we suddenly realized we were unprotected prey for any number of predators watching for unsuspecting tourists who had lost their way. The stench of the island landfill assaulted our senses, and circling birds of prey seemed waiting for our demise.

"Can't this thing go any faster?" I cried.

"I have it wide open," Steve assured me. "I'm trying to get us out of here as fast as I can." We were both terrified.

Finally, we did make it back to civilization. We threw off those helmets and ran across the plank to the ship as fast as our shaky legs could take us. In a matter of three hours, we had gone full circle.

After thinking about our trip from paradise to the landfill and back to paradise again, I saw a resemblance to life. Sometimes I feel as though I am living on the back side of the island. I look around, and garbage is all around me. I sense vultures circling just waiting for me to fall so they can pick me apart.

"Get me out of here!" I cry to God.

Just keep going, He seems to say. *Don't stop. Press on.*

We were not made for the garbage heap, and when we press on through those difficult days, we'll be back in paradise before we know it. The key is to keep going and not give up or settle.

So where are you today? Do you feel as though you're on the back side of the island with buzzards circling overhead? If so, God is encouraging you to keep going! Don't stop! Press on! Better days may be just around the bend.

Dear Lord, when I find myself in a dry and desolate place, help me keep moving forward until I'm back in the paradise of Your presence. In Jesus' name, amen.

ADDITIONAL SCRIPTURE READING: PSALM 42:1-11

94

A Dream Come True

How great is the love the Father has lavished on us,
that we should be called children of God!

1 JOHN 3:1

Once upon a time, not so very long ago or far away, a baby girl was born to parents who could not keep her. Even so, neither wanted to release her for adoption. So while the legal system shuffled her case back and forth, the baby girl grew into a toddler in a foster home.

Her care was certainly adequate, her physical needs were met, and she never went hungry. Her clothes, though not new, were never dirty. Her toys, though not her own, were always sufficient. This little girl was not mistreated or abused, and yet in her heart was a hollow space. She desperately wanted what she had never had—a mommy and a daddy of her very own.

Only a few doors down from the foster home lived a kind couple with a teenage son. The little girl needed a family, the family wanted a little girl, and the details of a trying and lengthy adoption were settled. And while this little girl received a wonderful mommy and an adoring big brother, it was her daddy who was extra special.

Ashley was two years old when she entered her new life. She was thin, pale, and clingy. By the time the adoption was finally complete, she was almost three. Ashley had never seen the ocean, eaten a Happy Meal, or slept in a bed in a room of her own.

A few months after the adoption, Ashley traveled to the beach for her first family reunion. She was overwhelmed with excitement and pride. She had received so much so fast, and it was hard to take it all in. Ashley asked everyone she met if they were part of her family.

"Are you my aunt?" "Are you my uncle?" "Are you my cousin?" She ran from person to person showering hugs and kisses on her newly acquired family. "I love you!" she told them. "I love you all!"

When her new daddy took her to McDonald's for the first time,

Ashley couldn't join in with the other children on the playground equipment. She was too busy asking important questions. "Do you have a daddy? I have a daddy! See, that's my daddy over there," she exclaimed with excitement and wonder. "Isn't he wonderful?"

"What's your name?" she asked. "My name is Ashley Jordan AMBROSE—just like my daddy. I'm named after my daddy!"

Five years later, tanned, transformed, and confident, Ashley again returned to the annual family reunion. This time she brought a scrapbook of pictures to share with anyone who would sit still long enough to listen.

"This is my story," she would say. "See, this is where I lived before Mommy and Daddy adopted me. They picked me out special. See, this is my room now—it's all my own. And these are my toys, and my *own* clothes, and here's a picture of my kitty, and one of my dog, and…"

Ashley has love overflowing for everyone, but no one is higher on her list than her daddy. He knows how to polish toenails, drip sand-castles, tie hair ribbons, hold her in the night—and he calls her his "little Princess."

When I think of Ashley, my heart melts in a puddle of love. See, it's not just Ashley's story. It is my story…and it is your story. We have been adopted into a loving family, and while I love my brothers and sisters in Christ, it is my Daddy who has a special place in my heart. God is our heavenly Father who loves us unconditionally, cares for us unendingly, and protects us unswervingly. He holds both you and me in the palm of His hand and calls us His "little Prince" or "little Princess."

Today, ponder the truth that God is your heavenly Father who loves you with an everlasting love. You are the apple of His eye.

⸎

Abba Father, I love You. Thank You for adopting me
into Your family and making me Your child. I pray I
will represent our family name (Christian) well as I go
about my daily activities today. In Jesus' name, amen.

ADDITIONAL SCRIPTURE READING:
EPHESIANS 1:1-14; 1 JOHN 3:1-2

95

Are You Spiritually Crippled?

Woman, you are set free from your infirmity.

LUKE 13:12

I was riding down the crowded streets of Mexico City in a cab when I saw her. She measured about four feet high, backed curved, bent at the waist at a ninety-degree angle, fingers gnarled and twisted shut. Like an upside-down chair, her face was parallel to the dirty sidewalk. Feet, dirt, trash. That was her view of the world. She shuffled alongside our car as we inched through the congested traffic. I saw her, but she did not see me. She could not see me. She just saw feet.

Sharon, look at My daughter, God seemed to say. *When you read about the woman with the crippled back, the one I healed in the synagogue, never again see her as a character in a story. See her as you see this woman now. Flesh and blood. Real and relevant. My daughter. Your sister.*

God reminded me once again that the women we read about in the Bible were real people—just like you and me. We must never forget that. Today, let's look at the woman with the crippled back in Luke 13:10-17. And while we might not be able to relate to being crippled physically, most of us can relate to being crippled emotionally. We see feet…people passing by going about their busy lives. We see dirt…the mistakes we've made through the years. We see trash…the pain inflicted on us by others and many times by our own poor decisions.

Jesus said, "Come to me, all you who are weary and burdened, and I will give you rest. Take my yoke upon you and learn from me, for I am gentle and humble in heart, and you will find rest for your souls" (Matthew 11:28-29). Rest for our souls. Isn't that what we all want? Like the woman with the crippled back, we may have "a spirit of infirmity" (Luke 13:11 NKJV), a sickness of the soul. That is an interesting way to explain her illness. More than just a crippled back, her spirit was crippled as well.

In *Jesus and Those Bodacious Women,* Linda Hollies brings this point home. "There are many spirits that can cause you to walk around in a bent-over state. They might be your color, your gender, your age, your marital state, your family, or they could be abuse, injustice, resentment, oppression, despair, loneliness, your economic state, or even a physical challenge. It makes no difference what has hurt you in the past, it makes no difference how old you were when the trauma affected your life, and it makes no difference what your wealth, position, or status is. For the evil one comes to steal, kill, and destroy and each one of us is a candidate for being bent and bowed."*

Bent and bowed. The weight of the world on our shoulders. Little by little. Day by day. Heaviness too difficult to bear. A spirit of infirmity. Crippled by shame, fear, pain, disappointment, depression, poverty, insecurity, inferiority, inadequacy, broken dreams. Satan, the one who orchestrates the spirit of infirmity, wants to cripple us into inactivity so that our walk becomes a shuffle. Our voice becomes a whisper. Our vision becomes a blur.

Who put the chains on her in the first place? Jesus said Satan had her bound (Luke 13:16). In reality, all sickness was ushered into the world when Adam and Eve believed Satan's lie over God's truth and ate the forbidden fruit.

For the 33 years that Jesus walked the earth, He was in a life-and-death struggle with evil. John tells us that the reason Jesus came was to destroy the devil's work (1 John 3:8). The battleground is the world and humans are the pawns of the evil one. This is about much more than physical healing. It is about spiritual freedom. And when Jesus said on the cross, "It is finished," it was. Now, because of Jesus' victory over the enemy through His death and resurrection, we are more than conquerors through faith in Him.

Don't miss this. Jesus said, "Woman, you are set *free* from your infirmity." The words paint a picture of chains and manacles falling from a prisoner's shackled body. Another translation says it this way: "Woman, you are *released* from your infirmity!" (Luke 12:13 AMP,

---

* Linda H. Hollies, *Jesus and Those Bodacious Women* (Cleveland, OH: Pilgrim Press, 1998), 44.

emphasis added). The irons of oppression that held her prisoner to her crippled frame gave way and fell at Jesus' feet as He unlocked the chains that had her bound.

Jesus came to set us free, and that freedom comes in many forms. Whatever Satan is using to bind you, Jesus came to free you. Free from… and free to. I can't say that enough. For far too long we've looked at freedom only in terms of what we are free from. But freedom encompasses so much more than a shedding of chains. Jesus set us free to live the abundant life by being all that He has created us to be and accomplishing all that He has planned for us to do. Setting the bent woman straight (literally) was only the beginning.

⌣

Dear Jesus, thank You for setting me free! Today, I choose to walk in that freedom and never be held captive by emotional chains again! In Your name, amen.

ADDITIONAL SCRIPTURE READING:
LUKE 13:10-17; ISAIAH 61:1-3

For As Long As We Both Shall Live

*A man will leave his father and mother
and be united to his wife, and they will become one flesh.*

GENESIS 2:24

F aces lined with years embraced cheek to cheek. Weathered hands
and arthritic fingers intertwined. Slow but steady gaits served as a
picture of enduring love in the winter of their lives. We were gathered
to celebrate my in-laws' sixtieth wedding anniversary. Like a rare treasure, their legacy of commitment and enduring love is the inheritance
they left to four grown children, five grown grandchildren, and a growing number of great-grandchildren.

Bruce and Mary Ellen grew up in the mountains of North Carolina
in the sleepy little hollow of Waynesville. From Bruce's first remem-
brance, he recalls the petite beauty with chestnut hair, a Coke-bottle
figure, and "plenty of book smarts." Back in the 1940s high school only
went through the eleventh grade, with an optional twelfth for those
who wanted to continue in their studies. Because Mary Ellen was one
grade behind, Bruce made the decision to stay one more year...to
continue his studies, of course. Bruce and Mary Ellen were a stunning
couple. His muscular build of 6' 4" towered over Mary Ellen's 5' 3". No
one was surprised when Bruce asked Mary Ellen to be his bride just a
few days after her graduation. On a beautiful November afternoon in
1943, they became man and wife. When they said the words "till death
do us part," they meant it. It was a vow made to one another and to
God, and the thought of anything other than a lifelong commitment
to each other was inconceivable...no matter what.

It was wartime when Bruce and Mary Ellen tied the knot, and 11
months after they were married, Bruce was shipped off to the Aleutian
Islands. For the next 18 months, the newlyweds corresponded through

the U.S. mail. There were no telephones, e-mails, or instant messaging. The communication of two hearts depended on prayer, pen, and paper. In one of his many letters, Bruce asked Mary Ellen to send him a photograph of her legs...which she did.

Never was a man so happy as when Bruce got off the bus, walked to Mary Ellen's grandparents' house, and saw his bride come bounding down the steps to rush into his hungry arms. Never again were they apart for an extended period of time.

Bruce went right to work when he arrived back in the United States, but he had a dream to go to college. Three years later, even though they now had a two-year-old baby girl in tow, Mary Ellen encouraged him to follow his dream. Bruce graduated from college with a master's degree in education, and for the next 39 years he served as a teacher, a coach, a high school assistant principal, and a junior high principal. Through the years, Mary Ellen had various jobs, but she retired after being with one company for twenty-five years. Together they raised four wonderful children...one of who became my husband on a beautiful summer day in August 1980. And that picture of Mary Ellen's legs? It was still in Bruce's wallet 60 years later.

I sat across the table from this amazing couple and watched as Mary Ellen lovingly wiped something from her husband's face. I saw tears pool in his eyes when he spoke about his bride. And though the years had changed their bodies, they were still a striking couple. Two ordinary people, serving an extraordinary God, offering us a rare and beautiful portrait of a marriage that lasts a lifetime.

Then I heard God say... *That's what I had in mind.*

Imagine with me for a moment. Think ahead 20, 40, 60 years. What do you see? Your marriage is becoming what it is going to be—and so much depends on you. No, building a wonderful marriage cannot be achieved by one party alone. It takes two. I take that back. It takes three: a woman who's committed to becoming the woman of her man's dreams; God, who longs to give her the power and creativity to do so; and a man who clings tightly to both.

Dear Lord, thank You for godly examples that have gone before us. Help us to have marriages that will leave a godly heritage for our children and grandchildren. That's the best inheritance of all. In Jesus' name, amen.

ADDITIONAL SCRIPTURE READING: EPHESIANS 5:21-33

97

The Redemption Center

*You know that it was not with perishable things such as silver
or gold that you were redeemed from the empty way of life
handed down to you from your forefathers, but with the
precious blood of Christ, a lamb without blemish or defect.*

1 PETER 1:18-19

When I was a little girl, my mother did her grocery shopping at White's Supermarket on the corner of Tarboro Street and Pearl. Other grocery stores were around, but White's gave out S&H Green Stamps with every purchase. On shopping days I watched as the cashier rang up my mom's purchases, pulling a lever with each entry. My mom's eyes lit up every time she heard the *cha-ching*, knowing that meant more stamps. When the total was tallied, the cash register spit out a stream of stamps, both large and small. We never put the stamps in the book right away. Mom stuffed them in a bag and waited until we had enough to make a whole day of it.

About every six months, Mom pulled down a brown paper grocery bag swollen with S&H Green Stamps from a shelf. She spilled its contents on the table and announced, "Okay, Sharon, it's time to paste the stamps."

For hours it was lick, stick, lick, stick, lick, stick. Large stamps represented dollars spent and three filled a page. Small stamps represented cents spent and 30 filled a page. I liked doing the dollar stamps.

After six months of collecting stamps and six hours of pasting them in books, my mom and I excitedly drove down to the S&H Green Stamp Redemption Center. With arms heavy laden, we plopped our day's work on the clerk's desk.

"Whatcha gonna get?" I'd ask as we strolled up and down the aisles of housewares.

"I don't know, honey," my mom would reply. "But it'll be something good."

After much consideration, Mom would decide on a treasure such as an electric can opener, a steam iron, or a shiny set of stainless steel mixing bowls. Oh, it was an exciting day to make a trip to the S&H Green Stamp Redemption Center and trade in our stamps for a special prize.

Thinking back on the event, God began to show me that this was a very simple picture of the word "redemption." It was to trade something in for something else, to take our stamps and trade them in (redeem them) for a prize—for something valuable. That's what God does with our lives. Because of Jesus' death on the cross, we have been redeemed. We have traded in our sin for His righteousness, our sorrow for His joy, our worry for His peace, and our bondage to sin for His freedom from it.

Today, ask God to show you a living example of an incident He has redeemed in your life. Ask Him to reveal how He has taken something seemingly bad and turned it into something amazingly good.

Dear Jesus, thank You for making the trade. Thank You for trading in Your life for mine. I don't deserve it— never could. But for a reason fully understood by God alone, You walked to that redemption center on the hill of Golgotha, and laid Your life down in exchange for mine. Thank You, Jesus. In Your name I pray, amen.

ADDITIONAL SCRIPTURE READING: ISAIAH 53:1-12; LUKE 1:58

98

God's Healing Salve

Forgive as the Lord forgave you.

COLOSSIANS 3:13

When I was a little girl, my grandmother kept a jar of Mentholatum salve ready at all times. No matter the nature of the ailment or the cause, Grandma pulled out the salve and rubbed the slimy goop all over my body. Got a headache? Mentholatum. Got a rash? Mentholatum. Got diabetes? Mentholatum. She believed it cured it all.

God has a salve as well. It's called forgiveness.

Forgiving those who have hurt or abused us is perhaps one of the most difficult aspects of healing for the soul, but without it I do not believe we can ever be free. Actually, without extending forgiveness, I believe the wound may not be able to heal at all. Each time we remember what was done to us, what was said and how it was said, how we were wronged but were oh so right—we pick at the scab of offense and reopen the wound.

"Unforgiveness can be likened to a parasite; it feeds on the anger and hurt of its host, finding its most satisfying nourishment in human pain. It thrives on the cycle of replayed scenes, recalled anguish, and rehashed justification for holding fast to grudges. Essentially, unforgiveness grows plump on our desire for revenge."*

While many of us don't exactly plan to exact revenge, we somehow think that holding on to unforgiveness is revenge enough. The irony is that the person whom we refuse to forgive most likely doesn't even care or know we're carrying the unforgiveness around. The only person being hurt when I choose not to forgive is…me. The only person being hurt when you choose not to forgive is…you. It is as if we are hitting our own heads against the wall in order to punish the other person.

The Greek word for forgiveness is *aphieme*. One meaning of the

---

* Diane Dempsey Marr, Ph.D., *The Reluctant Traveler* (Colorado Springs, CO: NavPress, 2002), 13.

word is to "let go of from one's power, possession, to let go free, to let escape."* It means to cut someone loose! So the opposite of forgiveness—unforgiveness—means to tie someone on. Just think about it. When we choose not to forgive, we tie the person to our backs and lug around the heavy burden of hate, bitterness, or revenge. No wonder some of us are not running the great race of life very well. It's difficult trying to run with someone or lots of someones tied to your back.

As we move along the journey of listening to God day by day, this is where many decide the terrain grows a bit too rugged to traverse. "That is too hard for me," the weary traveler moans. "I don't like that road," the rebellious sojourner protests. "Isn't there another way?" the reluctant traveler begs.

Unfortunately, forgiveness is the only path to freedom. Unforgiveness clogs our spiritual ears. Forgiveness opens the passageway for us to truly become women who listen to God.

Is there someone you need to cut loose today? Let's pray together.

~~

Dear God, this is hard, but today I choose to forgive _____ for _____. At this moment, I choose not to hold his (her) offense against him (her). I cut them loose from my back. I put him (her) into Your hands. I choose to forgive, even though I may not feel like it. I choose to forgive out of obedience. Give me the strength to not pick the unforgiveness back up and tie it on again. In Jesus' name, amen.

ADDITIONAL SCRIPTURE READING:
MATTHEW 6:13-15; COLOSSIANS 3:12-14; EPHESIANS 4:30-32

---

* Spiros Zodhiates, et al., eds., *The Complete Word Study Dictionary: New Testament* (Chattanooga, TN: AMG Publishers, 1992), 229.

99

Let's Give God a Round of Applause

Thanks be to God for his indescribable gift!

2 Corinthians 9:15

Steve and I boarded a cog train for a scenic ride to the top of Pike's Peak in Colorado Springs. It is the most visited mountain in North America—a hiker's paradise. But because going up and down my stairs at home is about as much hiking as I like to do, we opted for the train to chug us to the top. This stately mountain stands as a majestic backdrop to Colorado Springs and the Garden of the Gods rock formations. As we clicked along the 8.9 miles of railway, a tour guide pointed out various areas of interest and wildlife along the way. Suddenly, the train slowed to a crawl and a chorus of ooohs and aaahs rumbled through the cars. In hushed silence, we gazed at a herd of big horned sheep congregating to our right.

Six-foot male grayish-brown rams with white fluffy rumps gathered in a circle like spectators at a boxing match. Two males stood head-to-head in the center of the ring, eyeing each other with studied determination. Smaller female rams with diminutive spiked horns grazed nonplussed over to the side. It was mating season and the males were vying for the ladies' attention.

A loud crack filled the air as the two males ran toward each other and furiously butted heads. With front feet leaving the ground, the hefty rams twisted and turned interlocking horns until one retreated from battle. The sound of cameras clicking mixed with cracking rams horns as we dared not interfere with the ritual of thousands of years. Time and time again the males butted heads with one thing on their minds—the right to mate with the seemingly disinterested females grazing nearby. (Oh, we ladies can be so coy at times.)

After viewing this incredible display of God's creation, we broke out in cheers as the train continued its trek up the mountain. The tour guide enthusiastically shouted, "Folks, I want you to give yourself a big hand! I've never seen such a display on any of my trips up the mountain. Give yourselves a round of applause for seeing this magnificent sight today!" The entire coach broke out in wild cheers, applause, and congratulatory backslaps. Well, not the entire coach.

I looked at Steve and said, "Why in the world would we give ourselves applause? Why are these people clapping? We had absolutely nothing to do with it. God placed that in front of us for our enjoyment. He allowed a sneak peek at His divine creation. All we did was decide to get on the train."

Then I heard God speak to my heart. *Happens all the time.*

Oh, dear friend, God has given us an incredible gift of salvation. We don't earn it, merit it, or deserve it. If we could, it would not be referred to as a gift. Salvation is not something we should congratulate ourselves for. We actually have nothing to do with it. All we did was decide to get on the train. But praise God. He has promised us the ride of our lives filled with incredible displays of His splendor.

Today, let's give God a round of applause for all He's done in our lives. Let's thank Him for allowing us to get on heaven's train. And let's also pray that we will keep our eyes opened to marvelous displays of His creative genius along the way.

Creator God, thank You for opening my eyes to the truth. Without the power of the Holy Spirit working in my life, I know I would still be fumbling around in the darkness. Thank You for allowing me to take this incredible journey with You. In Jesus' name, amen.

ADDITIONAL SCRIPTURE READING: PSALM 147:1-20; 150:1-6

100

A Priceless Jewel

The Lord has chosen you to be his treasured possession.

DEUTERONOMY 14:2

To celebrate our twenty-fifth wedding anniversary, Steve and I took a land and sea excursion to Alaska. While on the cruise ship, we docked at various Alaskan fishing villages to mill around the shops and get a taste of Alaskan civilian life. When the boat docked at Juneau, it seemed everyone had lost their steam for wanderlust and opted to stay on the ship for the morning. But not me. I put on my jeans and a sweatshirt, donned my tennis shoes, and grabbed a credit card. Off I traipsed to explore the shops and do what I do best...look for bargains.

One particular store called Diamonds International beckoned me with bright red letters: "End of the Year Closeout Sale!" If I'm anything, I'm thrifty, so I decided this was the store for me.

"May I be of assistance?" The sleek saleswoman with a European accent gracefully swept her manicured hand across the glass case. "Are you looking for something in particular?"

"Yes," I answered. "I'm looking for a tanzanite slide for my necklace."

"Right this way," she answered as she elegantly glided across the room.

"Oh, I like this one," I said right away. "How much is it?"

"It retails for eighty-three, but our closeout price is forty-three." After using a coupon and having a little chat with the manager, the price was dropped to twenty-seven.

So I pulled my credit card from my pocket and the stone was mine. As the woman rang up the purchase, the store owner filled out an appraisal. I thought it was a bit strange to fill out an appraisal for such a small amount, but hey, what did I know? I took my purchase, stuffed it in my sweatshirt pouch, and headed out to peruse a few of the other jewelry stores.

I think I'll buy some earrings to match, I thought. As I went from store to store, I realized what a good deal I got at Diamonds International, so I decide to go back for another purchase. The wheeling and dealing followed the same pattern as before. They told me the suggested retail, then their closeout price, then the lower price because I was so special to them. Bottom line? Twenty-two. Sounded good to me. I gave the saleswoman my credit card again and the store owner began filling out another appraisal. But there was one small difference—this time I looked at the receipt before I signed it.

"Oh, I'm sorry, but you've made a mistake," I said. "This says the charge is twenty-two *hundred* dollars instead of twenty-two dollars."

"That is correct," she said.

"No, you said twenty-two," I said with a voice that had suddenly jumped two octaves. "You never said the word *hundred*!"

"Oh, no, mademoiselle. The earrings are twenty-two *hundred* dollars."

I dropped the receipt as though it had suddenly burst into flames. "I don't want them. There has been a big misunderstanding!" Then a sinking feeling hit as I put my hand in my sweatshirt pouch and felt my previous purchase.

"What did I just buy an hour ago?" I asked as I pulled the stone from my pouch.

"That was twenty-seven *hundred* dollars," she clarified.

"I thought it was twenty-seven dollars!" I shrieked. "You never said the word hundred! Not once!"

Thankfully, they took back the stone and credited my account. I ran back to the ship as fast as my little tennis shoes could carry me and promised to never go shopping without an escort again! (At least not in Alaska.) We all had a good laugh at my mistake.

When we got home, I told my son the story. He didn't laugh like everyone else. He just looked at me dumbfounded and said, "Mom, didn't you pick up on the clues?"

"Like what?" I asked.

"Like, the store you were in was called *Diamonds* International. The stone was set in 14 *karat gold*. It had little *diamonds* around it."

"Yeah, but they were very *little* diamonds!" I retorted.

"The manager wrote out an *appraisal*. He wouldn't do that for twenty-seven dollars."

"But it was an end-of-the-season closeout sale," I argued.

Steven just looked at me and shook his head.

You know, he was right. All along, there were hints that the tanzanite was much more valuable than twenty-seven dollars, and yet I refused to pay attention to the clues.

Oh, dear one, you are of great value to God. Have you been paying attention to the clues? You are His treasured possession. There is no closeout sale, end-of-the-year clearance, or discount coupon when it comes to your worth as a child of God. God loves and values you so much, He purposed for His only Son, whom He loved, to die on a rugged Roman cross to pay the penalty for your sin so that you could spend eternity with Him. He didn't have to do that, you know. But He did it because of your great worth to Him. You've been bought at a very high price…all sales final…no returns.

Do you know how much you are worth to God? Look for clues He gives you thoughout the day.

Dear Father, forgive me when I think of myself as less than I really am. I am a woman created in Your image, a masterpiece of grand design, a priceless treasure of great worth. In Jesus' name, amen.

ADDITIONAL SCRIPTURE READING: COLOSSIANS 1:9-29

About the Author

Sharon Jaynes is an international inspirational speaker and Bible teacher for women's conferences and events. She is the author of several books, including *What God Really Thinks About Women, Becoming the Woman of His Dreams, The Power of a Woman's Words, Your Scars Are Beautiful to God, Becoming Spiritually Beautiful, "I'm Not Good Enough"...and Other Lies Women Tell Themselves,* and *Becoming a Woman Who Listens to God.* Her books have been translated into several foreign languages and impact women around the globe. Her passion is to encourage, equip, and empower women to walk in courage and confidence as they grasp their true identity as a child of God and a co-heir with Christ.

Sharon is a cofounder of Girlfriends in God, a conference and online ministry that crosses denominational, racial, and generational boundaries to unify the body of Christ. To learn more visit www.girlfriendsinGod.com.

Sharon and her husband, Steve, have one grown son, Steven. They call North Carolina home.

Sharon is always honored to hear from her readers. You can contact her directly at Sharon@sharonjaynes.com or at her mailing address:

Sharon Jaynes
PO Box 725
Matthews, NC 28106

To learn more about Sharon's books and speaking ministry or to inquire about having her speak at your next event, visit www.sharonjaynes.com

Other Books
by Sharon Jaynes

The Power of a Woman's Words

The Power of a Woman's Words is for every woman who desires to use her words to build up rather than tear down, to encourage rather than discourage, to cheer rather than jeer. It is for all who desire to have more control over that mighty force called the tongue.

The Power of a Woman's Words
Interactive Study Guide

This engaging, interactive workbook for Sharon's book and the companion DVD series offers you exciting biblical examples, contemporary insights, and questions to help you embrace lessons on using godly words and perspective to inspire strength, joy, and purpose in yourself and others.

The 5 Dreams of Every Woman…
And How God Wants to Fulfill Them

Sharon shares powerful stories alongside biblical, compassionate guidance to help restore women's hope in love, marriage, motherhood, purpose, and more. You will learn to give your longings and brokenness to God and delight in His renewal and remarkable dreams for you. Study questions included.

What God Really Thinks About Women

With her trademark biblical perspective, Sharon explores how God interacted with and cared for women of the Bible and uncovers surprising insights she is excited to share with her readers today—God has great dreams for them and continues to transform women, heart by heart, in deeply personal ways.

What God Really Thinks About Women
Bible Study Guide

Sharon presents an engaging, interactive companion study guide to *What God Really Thinks About Women.* Passage explorations, reflective questions, and personal insights about Jesus' encounters with women in the Bible reveal how God transforms, heals, and interacts with us today.

Becoming a Woman Who Listens to God

Women can find themselves overwhelmed, and they often long for time away from it all so they can hear God's still, small voice. Using biblical wisdom and insights from her own life, Sharon invites you to explore answers to the heart cry, "How can I hear the voice of God?"

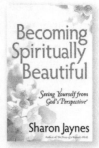

Becoming Spiritually Beautiful

In *Becoming Spiritually Beautiful,* popular author Sharon gently shares how becoming spiritually beautiful is something full of promise and possibilities. Spiritual beauty brings new beginnings, fresh faith, and the hope of a beauty unique in the universe.

"I'm Not Good Enough"...and Other Lies Women Tell Themselves

Sharon looks at the common lies women tell themselves and shows them how they can replace those lies with Truth. Her book is a handy reference tool that will help women renew their minds and think God's thoughts rather than be swayed by the enemy's deceptions.

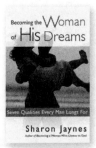

Becoming the Woman of His Dreams

This book is a thoughtful look at the wonderful, unique, and God-ordained role a woman has in her husband's life. Sharon offers seven key qualities every wife should strive for.

Your Scars Are Beautiful to God

Sharon shares with women how their emotional scars can lead to restoration. Encouraging chapters and inspirational stories reveal how women can give their past pains over to the One who turns hurts into hope.

Building an Effective Women's Ministry

This unique yet practical how-to manual offers a wide range of help to women, from those just starting out to those who have a thriving ministry but could use a fresh idea or two.

A Woman's Secret to a Balanced Life

Coauthored with Lysa TerKeurst, this essential book offers seven vital ways any Christian woman can prioritize her life more effectively.

To learn more about other Harvest House books
or to read sample chapters, log on to our website:

www.harvesthousepublishers.com

HARVEST HOUSE PUBLISHERS

EUGENE, OREGON